DARN IT!
The History and Romance of Darners

by
Wayne Muller

Photography by
Stuart Muller

Published by

P.O. Box 69
Gas City, IN 46933

ISBN: 0-89538-072-2
©Copyright 1995
Wayne Muller

LAYOUT AND DESIGN
Amy Van Hoosier

Dedication

To the hundreds of collectors, antique dealers, librarians, curators, publishers, authors, manufacturers, distributors, retailers and friends who have gladly and most generously shared their knowledge, experience and expertise to enhance this work.

But especially to Mary Muller who has lovingly shared her caring, concern and support to encourage and inspire this writer.

Table of Contents

Chapter 1	The Romance of Darning The Utilitarian Art	5 - 9
Chapter 2	The History of Stockings Our Newest Garment	10 - 11
Chapter 3	The Evolution of Stockings From Pelts to Panty Hose	12 - 15
Chapter 4	Darners The Ultimate, Infinite Collectibles	16 - 32
Chapter 5	Catalog of Darners In Living Color with Value Guide	33 - 151
Acknowledgements		152 - 154
Bibliography		155 - 157
Index		158 - 160

Pricing Note

The values in this book should only be used as a guide. They are not intended to set prices which vary due to local demand, condition and availability. Auction and dealer prices also vary greatly. Neither the author nor the publisher assumes responsibility for any losses that might be incurred as a result of consulting this guide.

DON'T MISS

THIS NEW HUMOROUS CARTOON BOOK "A PRICELESS GUIDE TO THE ANTIQUE BUSINESS", THIS IS A LOOK AT OUR BUSINESS "THE ANTIQUE BUSINESS" SEE YOURSELF, YOUR DEALERS, YOUR CUSTOMERS, YOU WILL SEE FUNNY EVENTS THAT WILL BRING BACK FOND MEMORIES.

1069

This book has 128 pages of cartoons. This book was drawn by well known illustrator Patrick Campbell. Buy a few and place them by your cash register or check out spot. Wonderful impulse item. You must try at least one. (We recommend a pile of 6-8 for impulse display.) 8 1/2" x 5 1/2", B/W, Paperback.

FOR A $5.95 STICKER PRICE THIS IS A STEAL! (Ha! Ha!)

$5.95 + $2.00 Shipping for the first book 40¢ each additional
Send Check or Money order to:
L-W Book Sales, P.O. Box 69, Gas City, IN 46933
Or Call 1-800-777-6450 for Visa, Mastercard & C.O.D. Orders Only!

Chapter 1

The Romance of Darning: The Utilitarian Art

There was a time when no proper household would be without one. It was as common as the sad iron, the button hook and the antimacassar. It lay unobtrusively in the sanctuary of the sewing basket, the sewing machine drawer or the darning bag. A mundane, humble workaday tool that was a needed and much used implement, utilized not only by the lady of the house, but also in many cases by the children and even the man of the house.

Today, although it is very rare to see one being used, there are undoubtedly millions of them still in existence, perhaps sequestered along with the sewing bird and the spinning wheel; but most of all, treasured by collectors all over the world.

It was the ubiquitous and essential darner, the handy little gadget that was used as an aid in the darning of holes in stockings, gloves and garments - back in the days when people darned holes instead of throwing them away.

Not only were the holes darned, but they were darned with great skill and pride. Young girls, and boys too, were trained in the art, sometimes by their mothers or grandmothers, sometimes by instructors in "Home Economics" classes, teachers at boarding schools or nuns in girls academies.

Sewing was also taught in many of the private schools for young ladies in the early 1800's, such as the Young Ladies Seminary in Bethleham, Pennsylvania and the Westtown School in Chester County, Pennsylvania.

Anna Green Winslow attended Madame Smith's Sewing School where, according to her diary, she learned spinning, plain sewing, and mending. On March 9, 1772, she records: "I sew'd on the bosum of unkle's shirt, mended two pairs of gloves, mended for the wash two handkerchiefs (one cambrick) sewed on half a border of a lawn apron of aunts." February 22, 1772: "I have spun 30 knots of lining yearn, and (partly) new footed a pair of stockings."*

England's compulsory education act of 1870, required that children be taught the domestic skills, especially since many of them would be employed in the households of the aristocrats and the wealthy.

One of the instruction books for the teachers of these classes had this to offer: "If wisely taught, it (darning) develops the thrifty dispositions, encourages habits of neatness, cleanliness, order, management and industry and may truly be considered a moral and refining influence both in the home and in the school. Patching, darning, knitting and homemade garments are all ways and means of economizing." The manual also included this: "Children must learn on waste knitting (to darn) but practice as soon as possible on a garment. Encourage the girls to bring to school worn socks and stockings in clean condition to show them how to hold these while darning and suggest the shape that will be best for thin places. Darning, to be perfect, requires much practice."

In her book *The Complete Encyclopedia of Needlework,* Therese de Dillmont wrote: "The mending of clothing, underwear, and house linen, though wearisome, is nevertheless very necessary, and no woman should be ignorant of the best methods of doing it. There is as much merit in knowing how to repair the damage caused by wear and tear or by accident, as in the perfect making of new articles."

Sometime after 1912, when the Girl Scouts of the United States was established, some young girls learned how to darn stockings while earning their patches in "Sewing," or perhaps in "Textiles and Fibers." The Girl Guides were established in England in 1909 and in Canada in 1910. Some girls may have discovered the joys of darning while earning their "Home" emblems.

Darning was not an activity reserved exclusively for the less than affluent. On the contrary, it was considered, even in most prosperous households, to be the "proper" thing to do. Although there might be maids or live-in girls, the ladies of the household still did some darning. It gave them a sense of accomplishment, achievement and satisfaction.

As de Tillmont noted: ". . . repairing damage caused by wear and tear is an art, quite as valuable as that of skillfully fashioning new articles."

*(Antiques of American Childhood by Katharine Morrison McClinton ©1970, Clarkson N. Potter, Inc. Publ. NY)

After all, thrift - along with patience - is a virtue. And virtue, or at least the appearance thereof, was a quality much desired and admired. The ladies, and other darnees as well, would have been a joy to today's "Waste Not, Want Not" ecologists.

Even today, near the beginning of the 21st century, some people darn, not because they need to economize, but rather because of the gratification darning gives them. Robert Epstein, Berkeley, California psychotherapist, writing in *East West Natural Health: The Guide to Well-Being,* puts it this way, ". . . I do derive great satisfaction from mending things, and I'm beginning to think putting a household object back into working order is a significant act. I especially like to mend socks. Please think twice before throwing your socks away. By mending them, you may also be mending the holes in your life, and creating a treasure."

Why Palistine Liberation Organization Chief, Yasser Arafat, still darns his socks was not indicated, but his young wife said in late 1993: "When you marry a man who's been a bachelor until age 60, there are habits you can't change. He even darns his own socks and sews buttons. He sews better than I do."

There was another equally compelling aspect to darning which had to do with personal relationships. That was the concept that darning was a demonstration of devotion. A darner from Switzerland bears a legend in German that translates approximately to this: "The greatest love is if you promise to darn my socks daily," a concept which today's modern woman might not find tolerable, it was practical and acceptable in its time.

The Norwegians apparently had no problem with this concept. A Norse adage states:
"Love your man
   and darn his hoses
And you will
   forever dance on roses."

It is known that Eleanor Roosevelt, wife of Franklin D. Roosevelt, President of the United States for 1932 to 1945, learned to darn stockings at an early age. In the Eleanor Roosevelt Gallery of the Franklin D. Roosevelt Library and Museum in Hyde Park, New York there is a display of some of her sewing and darning equipment. Mounted on a plaque is a celluloid set consisting of a stocking darner, a bodkin and decorated thimble. And in a sewing stand nearby are two more stocking darners. The placard in the display states: "Throughout her life Mrs. Roosevelt was seldom without knitting or sewing to pick up whenever possible. She recalled in later years that when she was about six her nurse taught her to darn socks. If she made a mistake the nurse would cut out the yarn, thus making the hole larger, and have her start again."

Even thought their primary interest was in sewing machines, the Singer Sewing Machine Company, did not hesitate to offer instructions on hand darning. An early Singer Sewing Book included these instructions:

"Use a darning ball to darn socks and small embroidery hoop for flat work. Use a fine needle and do not knot the end of the thread. Darn the sock over the darning ball, or place the flatwork in the hoop. Make small running stitches, beginning about 1/4 inch beyond the edge of the hole; work across to the opposite side, extending the stitches 1/4 inch beyond the hole. Work back and forth, keeping the lines of stitching and the threads across the hole parallel and evenly spaced until the hole is covered. Then turn and work across the threads, weaving alternately over and under in parallel lines until the repair is completed. Be careful not to draw the threads taut; this will cause the work to pucker. Fasten the threads on the underside. Press."

In spite of the fact that this publication carried instructions for darning by hand it also includes instructions to darn with the Singer Sewing Machine with the special Stocking Darner attachment.

Youngsters were taught to darn just as they were taught all of the domestic arts such as cooking, baking, laundering, ironing and sewing. They learned darning at the same age as they learned to make samplers, which would have been around 7 to 10 years of age.

Illustrative of these early-age activities are the "Sunbonnet Babies" who became popular in 1902 in the Sunbonnet Babies Primer stories written by Eulalie Osgood Grover and illustrated by Bertha Cooper. These little tykes appear to be about six years old and they are performing all the household chores on the prescribed days of the week: Monday, laundry; Tuesday, ironing; Wednesday, mending; Thursday, mopping and window washing; Friday, sweeping and house cleaning; Saturday, baking; Sunday, resting. On Wednesday, the "mending" day, one of the little girls is darning a stocking.

Darners and darning were a popular theme for Valentines, and Birthday, Anniversary and Get-Well cards, as well as childrens' books - note the problems of Holly Hobby as she juggles her sewing basket and darner while trying to dislodge the sleeping cat from her stool while the kitten worries her ball of yard; or Janet, in the *Picture and Rhyme Book,* dismayed by a hole in a heel bigger than her hand.

Plate A
Sunbonnet Babies

Plate B
The Days of Holly Hobby

Plate C
The Picture and Rhyme Book "Janet"

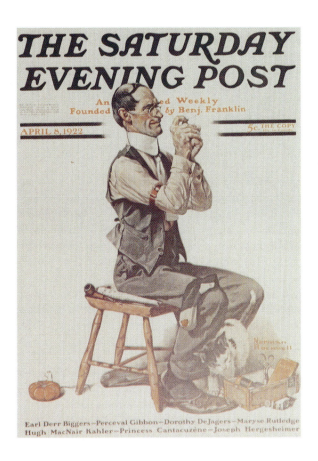

Plate D
Saturday Evening Post

Adults were not exempt either, as shown in a Norman Rockwell cover for the *Saturday Evening Post.* A red darner shows through the hole in the white toe of a black sock.

Although most of the emphasis in this volume is on darning stockings, all types of clothing were darned and mended. Elbows of sweaters were darned. Knees of trousers were patched. Underwear, shirts, blouses, night gowns, blankets, bed spreads, table cloths, napkins, towels, in fact any kind of material that could be salvaged, was restored and recycled by the proverbial "stitch in time."

One stratagem used to motivate young girls to discover the joys of needle working was to provide them with all the sewing accessories that Mother had. She would receive needles, spools of thread, scissors, thimble, darner, emery ball, pincushion, and perhaps even an odd bodkin, all probably contained in a fancy sewing box, which might not have been a "box" at all, but rather a basket or bag.

But in any event, now she was equipped to emulate Mother and learned to do needlework, particularly darning, all the while believing it was play. And many a youngster in the days of "Use it up, wear it out; Make it do, or do without," earned her weekly allowance by performing the chore of doing the family darning.

Gertrude Whiting, in her book *Old Time Tools & Toys of Needlework,* says this about her early darning days: "When I was little and complained of feeling poorly, I was allowed to stay home from school; but in that case, I must sit quietly darning my brother's socks. Needless to say, I did not pretend any false ailments!"

It should be noted that there were two basic types of needlework. One was "utilitarian," to create or preserve necessary items. This would include such activities as making rugs, knitting sweaters and repairing garments. The other type of needlework was "decorative" such as embroidering, needlepointing and crocheting.

Some needlework was a combination of utilitarian and decorative types, such as making quilts which were both useful and attractive. But whether utilitarian, decorative or a combination of both, needlework - or "busywork" as it was sometimes called - was and still is for many, a form of relaxation and recreation.

In many instances, some of the ladies in the "sewing circle" were not doing fancy embroidery. They were darning. And good darning, although it was the strictly utilitarian aspect of needlework, was indeed considered to be "fancy" sewing. To be able to make a smooth, thin, soft darn that would not irritate the wearer's foot was an art, and required a high level of skill.

The comprehensive definition of "darning" is to mend by interweaving thread or yarn across a hole or tear in a garment and to imitate the texture of the article by sewing a network of stitches across the space. This type of darning took time to perform and required concentration. It could be tedious, but the persons doing the darning eased the monotony by meditation, conversation, or listening to someone else read aloud. In later years, listening to the talking machine or still later, the radio, helped relieve the tedium.

There were other types of so-called "darning" that were practiced by some darnees. One consisted of running a thread around the perimeter of the hole, somewhat like a noose, and then pulling the hole closed. Another type of darning, called "ridging," was achieved by simply holding the edges of the hole together and overcasting with long wrapping stitches.

Gertrude Whiting writes in *Old Time Tools & Toys of Needlework:* "A friend of mine who, during the World War, acted as a farmerette, was told by the farmer's wife to darn her husband's socks. She proceeded to do so in the usually accepted manner of weaving her needleful of thread under and over, but was brusquely stopped and told not to waste time! The wife explained that the thread should be run round the hole in the stocking and pulled or drawn up; then the two opposite edges of the opening should be overcast together in a ridge. While these sorts of darning did save time, they had some very definite disadvantages. They created lumps and ridges which could cause great discomfort to the wearer. Besides, if done too often, one could wind up with a very short sock.

Mr. Henry Owen of England had a different idea of the proper way to mend stockings. In 1859 he applied for a patent covering a design for stockings in which the damaged section could be easily removed and replaced by a complete new section. He stated "This invention relates to a novel mode of repairing (by means of piecing instead of darning) stockings and socks, and every description of hose manufacture.

"By this invention the tedious process of darning is superseded by a peculiar arrangement for piecing without overlapping. By this arrangement it is intended in the manufacture of hose, half hose, and all such articles of dress, to construct and prepare seams of selvedge courses about the foot, that is, across various parts of the foot, namely, above, underneath, and on the foot so manufactured, about or above the foot, that the whole or its parts, namely, the heel or sole, or toe parts may be removed at the seams or selvedge which will not drop, or ravel, or loosen the fabric, or require taking up in order to make it secure. The purpose of this arrangement in the manufacture of hose is that the seamed parts, edges, or selvedge courses in the foot shall correspond, when the worn parts are cut away and removed, with new pieces made to replace them, and be so adapted to join such new parts as not to need overlapping in order to secure them, but fitting exactly and corresponding selvedge to selvedge, (that is, the selvedge of the new piece to the selvedge of the hose from which the worn part has been cut away), that the seam formed by the joining of both shall be even and flat, and quite easy and imperceptible to the foot." Whew!

The consensus about this invention among people who mended stockings is lost in the murky past. However, socks were still being "darned," as opposed to being "pieced," well into the 20th century. Sometimes stockings were darned even though they did not have any holes. This was "preventative medicine," the purpose of which was to forestall the development of holes. Even before being worn, new stockings were darned in the most vulnerable areas to strengthen them and thus delay their wearing through. This practice was particularly prevalent in items of shortages, such as war time, and during economic lows.

Most darning was done using "Darning Floss." Cotton and Mercerized-finish darning floss were most common, although there was also silk floss. Each thread had up to four strands of floss which could be separated and the number of strands used depended on the weight of the material being darned. Cotton was generally used for the heavier material and silk or Mercerized-finish floss was used for lighter material such as silk and lisle and sometimes a perfectly suitable substitute for silk floss was a strand of human hair!

de Dillmont, in writing about invisible darning or fine-drawing, stated: "The latter was done with human hair - red or white hairs being the strongest - which had been carefully cleansed from grease! We are assured that the sharpest eye will fail to detect a rent carefully darned in this manner!"

The ultimate compliment that could be said of a lady who darned was "She does a fine darn." This was not idle flattery. Unfortunately, some ladies were not trained to darn and did not attempt it until they became brides, and the results could be hazardous to the health of the new marriage. The results of a rough, thick, lumpy "darn" were blisters, chafing and soreness and a very grouchy wearer.

Some people who darned felt a strong compulsion to darn on the "right" side. That is, to darn from the outside of the stocking so that the darn would look nice and smooth, presumably on the premise that one never knew when one might have to take off one's shoes in public. This was the same line of reasoning that prompted mothers to insist that their children never wear holey underwear. "What if you got in an accident and had to go to the hospital?"

But from a practical standpoint, it was better to turn the stocking inside out and darn from the inside so that the darn would feel nice and smooth against the toes or heel, rather than to be concerned with how it looked.

The knot was another "no no." All thoughtful instructions on darning was emphatic that the darning thread not be knotted. A knot could be the cause of a blister. Instead the thread was to be made fast by a sequence of running stitches.

Many a time the podiatrist recommended that his patient throw away all darned stockings, or at least have them darned by someone who knew how to perform an acceptable darn.

On an even more serious note, there is the story of a lady who was told specifically by her doctor not to ever darn her diabetic husband's stockings or allow him to wear any that had holes, tears or darns in them. Instead, he emphasized the importance of immediately disposing of any sock that developed a hole or tear. He explained that a rough darn or hole could cause irritation which could result in a sore and, because one of the characteristics of diabetes is slow healing, gangrene could develop with serious consequences. So the importance of doing a good darn was much more that just cosmetic or just for comfort. It also could affect the physiological functioning of the foot.

Essential to the achievement of a good " darn" was good eyesight and proper light. Many people, especially in the preelectric light days, preferred not to darn in the evening, given the poor visibility afforded by candles, oil lamps, kerosene lamps or gas lights. Yet, for many homemakers, the evening time - after supper was over, the table was cleared, the dishes washed and dried, the children settled at their homework - was about the only time of the entire day that they could sit down and relax, usually with the day's mending.

So the fertile minds of the inventors sprang into action and came up with lighted darners, powered by batteries and later by electricity. Also to help deal with this problem, darners came in different colors - dark darners for use with light colored stockings and light darners for use with dark colored stockings - so as to provide contrast.

While most people darned with the same colored thread as the color of the stocking, some preferred to use contrasting colors - as does the Norman Rockwell character on *The Saturday Post* cover, who is using black thread to darn the white toe. This concept was carried to the outer extreme by one lady, which resulted in her husband eventually insisting that she use matching thread in darning his socks. Being bored with using black thread on black socks and white thread on white socks, she had darned them in brilliant colors such as red, green, orange, blue or yellow. He didn't mind until he joined a health club and took off his shoes in the locker room. He could not tolerate being the "laughing stock" of the club.

Chapter 2

The History of Stockings: Our Newest Garment

Unlike the puzzlement of which came first - the chicken or the egg - we know that the stocking came before the darning egg. Yet the time when the first stocking arrived on the clothing scene has not been precisely established.

The fact of the matter is that all clothing, including stockings, did not suddenly "arrive," but rather developed in stages over long periods of time. However, the stocking was one of the last articles of clothing to be developed.

People wore some form of coverings over their bodies and their heads, and some type of primitive shoes or boots, long before they got around to stockings. Of course, for perhaps millions of years, mankind did not wear any clothes. But as man evolved and moved into different environments, the need for different types of protection arose and the wearing of outer garments began.

But there were many reasons why mankind wore, or wears today, additional accoutrements. Climate is always a factor. People who lived in tropical zones had little need for protection from the elements. Conversely, those living in the less-than-temperate zones, such as the Asiatic immigrants who came to the North American continent by way of the Bering Strait and Alaska had very acute needs for protection from the weather.

Another consideration was as adornment, and to make themselves more attractive. From primitive peoples who ornamented themselves with feathers, shells, animal claws, teeth and skins - to modern folks in their manufactured clothes and footwear-there has always been the element of fashionable adornment. Historically, it was usually the males who dressed for embellishment, such as the Beau Brummells with powdered wigs and feathered hats, but later it became the ladies who dressed for chicness and attractiveness.

It has been suggested that some people began wearing clothes because of a natural inclination toward modesty. If this were a factor, it probably arose later. And yet, there were primitive people, living in temperate and tropical climates, who wore loin cloths and other clothing. This may have been because the groin represented strength and the center of reproduction, and thus was to be protected and esteemed. Today, there are people who believe that modesty about the human body is false modesty and the nudists have no qualms about going without any clothing in the appropriate environment.

Another possible reason for the development of clothing may have been for disguise. Primitive man may have discovered that he became a more successful hunter if he cloaked himself in animal skins; just as modern day hunters and soldiers often wear camouflage suits.

There was also the element of superstition. Some natives believed that wearing the skin from certain animals, such as the lion, gave them the bravery and attributes of that animal. Others believed that clothing, particularly the skins of animals, was a defense against curses and evil spirits.

In any event, stockings were among the last items of wearing apparel to materialize. There is evidence that Neolithic man as early as 15,000 years ago in Russia, knew how to weave, but there is nothing to indicate that he wove, or wore, stockings. As early as 6,000 years ago, the Lake Dwellers of Switzerland had tools for spinning and weaving of cloth, but there is no sign that they ever made stockings.

Cloth and tools for spinning and weaving have been found in the graves from the Bronze Age, 3500 to 1100 BC, but no clue that they were used to make stockings. In fact, as late as September of 1991, the preserved body of a Bronze Age mountain climber estimated to be over 5000 years old was uncovered in the snow, high on the Austrian/Italian border. He was wearing a pair of primitive leather shoes, but no stockings. Instead, his shoes were stuffed with grass to preserve warmth. Other cultures are known to have used for padding and insulation in their footwear vegetable fibers such as moss and lichen and animal fibers such as wool and fur.

The Bible alludes to weaving and fine linen, and makes reference to "shoes," but does not mention stockings. Nor does the Torah. Also the Egyptians wove fabrics and linen, as the wrappings of mummies prove, but the ancient mummies did not wear stockings, although later ones did.

A "sort-of" type of stockings were wrappings or bindings, made of woven cloth or leather, often in several different colors, that were wound around the shins. But the first record of what we would consider the forerunner of our stocking that covers the foot as well as the leg occurs in a writing by a Greek poet named Hesiod who lived in the last half of the 8th century B.C.

In a poem called "Works and Days," he counsels the farmers in his village to "Put on your feet stout shoes, close fitting, made of the hide of a slaughtered ox . . . and let them be thickly lined in PILOI." Piloi meant "felt" and was derived from the Greek word for "hair," because before they knew how to spin and weave, the Greeks made a form of cloth by matting, or "felting," the hair or fur of animals, particularly sheep and goats. Piloi has been translated to mean "felt socks," and may well be the first written word suggesting the idea of a sock.

The Romans borrowed the concept of stockings from the Greeks, and by 100 AD had a sock called an "UDO" which, although of felt, skins or woven cloth, was similar to our present day socks. Later, between 300 and 400 AD, full length stockings, called "UDONES" were developed and were in common usage by the Romans. These stockings covered the foot and calf, and extended above the knee. They were cut from pieces of cloth, fitted and sewn with a seam up the back. Generally they were made of linen and later of silk. They were worn not only by ordinary citizens, but were also considered an essential part of the vestments of the Roman Catholic clergy as a sign of purity.

While hosiery as we know it today has its roots in Greece and Rome, in the course of its evolution throughout history, the stocking has undergone many changes in form and fabric.

Chapter 3

The Evolution of Stockings: From Pelts to Panty Hose

From their primitive beginnings to the present time, stockings have experienced mutations and modifications in the materials from which they were made, in the way they were fabricated, and in their style. The earliest "stockings" were probably made from animal skins. By the time mankind got around to thinking about stockings, long after the age of the dinosaurs, there was a copious quantity of smaller animals with softer, more flexible pelts, suitable for making reasonably wearable socks. Goat skin was used in the making of the Roman socks called UDO, later in the first century A.D. Leather stockings continued to be made and advertised in America in the 1700's.

Another ancient fabric was felt. Long before man learned to weave or knit, he had discovered that the hair of animals, when moistened and compacted, would cling together to form a matted material. Later, the hair of sheep and goats, especially Angora goats, and Angora rabbits became the material of choice in the making of felt. The Roman UDO, in addition to being made of leather or woven, were also made of felt, and even today felt appears in many commonplace articles such as hats and slippers.

As mentioned earlier, sometime in the Neolithic era, possibly as early as 15,000 years ago, man had learned that by interlacing strands of fiber he could create a fabric. He had learned to weave. Mostly he wove with vegetable fibers, flax being probably the first vegetable fiber known to man. It was from this early weaving of flax that linen derived, and linens more than 3,500 years old have been discovered in Egyptian tombs.

Linen became a major fabric for the making of stockings and by 300 to 400 A.D. linen stockings had become a mandatory part of the vestments of the Roman Catholic clergy and linen was the favorite stocking fabric of the general population.

Other vegetable fibers from which fabrics were woven were bast and hemp. They tended to be rough and were used more for cloth, matting and rope. Hemp is still being grown today, for legal and for illegal purposes, because it didn't take mankind - ingenious creature that he is - long to discover that hemp, or cannabis, in addition to fiber, also produced marijuana and hashish.

From India came cotton, the most important of the vegetable fibers. Hundreds of years B.C., the people of India were weaving fabrics out of cotton. It was thought of as "wood from trees" and the German name for it reflects that. It is called "Baumwolle" - baum for tree and wolle for wool.

It was cotton that became the savior of the American South many years later when tobacco prices dropped, the market for indigo declined and the rice crops were not doing well. And it became "King Cotton" when Eli Whitney invented the cotton engine, or "gin." Cotton cloth could now be manufactured considerably cheaper, much to the chagrin of woolen producers, chiefly English, who fought the progress of cotton vigorously, but to no avail. Cotton was used in the production of stockings into modern times and in the 1900's it was often Mercerized, that is, treated with a chemical which gave it a "silkier" sheen and improved its tensile strength.

But what became the real pet of the "natural" stocking fabrics was silk. Although the raising of silkworms and processing of their cocoons into silk is thought to have originated in China in 2640 B.C. - due to a fortuitous discovery by Xi Lingshi, the wife of Emperor Huang Ti - it was not until 550 A.D., or over 3000 years later that it became known to the western world. After all, the emperor had mandated that anyone revealing the secret would be put to death by very unpleasant means.

The revelation finally came when two Persian Christian monks prevailed on Emperor Justinian I of the Eastern Roman Empire, who rewarded them richly for bringing the silk making process to the West. Justinian heartily agreed and the monks returned to China, smuggled silkworm eggs out in their bamboo walking sticks and trudged back to Constantinople, where they taught the Eastern Romans the secrets of producing silk. But in spite of the fact that it was precious and hard to come by, silk became the most desirable fabric for fancy stockings. In 1560, Queen Elizabeth was so delighted with her first pair of silk stockings, which were knit for her by her knitting lady Mrs. Montague, that she stated: "I like silk stockings so well . . . so pleasant, fine and delicate. Henceforth, I will wear no more cloth stockings." The desirability of silk was such that in 1608 King James I had 10,000 black mulberry trees planted in England with the aim of becoming a silk producing nation. However the endeavor was doomed from the start; he had planted black mulberry trees and the silkworms favored white mulberry leaves.

Many years later when growers in the American South, especially Georgia, tried to cash in on the demand for silk, as they had for cotton, they met with the same lamentable results. The climate was not suitable; the silkworm would not perform satisfactorily; although some types of silkworms ate different leaves such as oak leaves, the ideal white mulberry trees, from which the best silk derived, would not flourish there; workers who were skilled in silk production were virtually nonexistent and very expensive. So the silk producing industry in America died aborning. However, the passion for silk stockings did not wane until the middle of the 20th century, and then the hero, or villain - depending on your point of view - was man-made fabrics.

In the early part of the 1900's, rayon was developed, and although used in both men and women's hosiery, it did not achieve lasting popularity for women's stockings because it was not "elastic" enough and tended to sag. Later, other man-made fabrics included Dacron, Orlon, Dynel and Acrilan. These have some applications for men's and children's hosiery, but not so much for the ladies.

But the sensational event that really shook the hosiery world was proclaimed on October 27, 1938. E.I. du Pont de Nemours announced their new synthetic super-polymers, "surpassing in strength and elasticity any previously known textile fibers." This new family of materials was given the general term of 'Nylon'. Although du Pont orchestrated the introduction of this remarkable new product to the public as painstakingly as possible in an attempt to avoid any problems or favoritism, the day nylon stockings became available in the stores produced a near frenzy among some ladies who had waited in line for hours for stores to open and then stormed the hosiery department with exceeding enthusiasm.

But World War II brought an abrupt halt to this euphoria. Nylon went to war - in the form of parachutes, belts, webbing, cord for tires and a hundred other uses. Nylon stockings were collected along with pots and pans and scrap metal to go into the war effort. This left fabrics of rayon and wool for stockings. These fabrics were just barely tolerable in the winter time, but in warm, humid summer they were not even tolerably bearable.

However, in the early 1940's, except for the "bobby soxers," who delighted in mismatched socks and shoes, it was not considered proper for the well dressed lady to go bare legged. But again, mankind's ingenuity rode to the rescue. This time in the form of leg makeup; stockings one poured out of a bottle. A woman could apply her bottled stockings at home, complete with a seam up the back drawn with an eyebrow pencil, or she could patronize a "leg bar" at any number of leading department stores, where you could get a pedicure, hair removed, leg massage and professionally applied makeup stockings. It was claimed by the manufacturers that this miracle of modern science looked like silk, wouldn't rub off, wouldn't stain clothes and would last for three days.

On the other hand, it was also recommended that the wearer refrain from indulging in a hot bath, but rather confine her ablutions to a lukewarm shower. Also, many a man was discouraged from dancing too closely when he discovered his partner's stockings had rubbed off on his white flannel slacks. However, as the formulae evolved, the problems lessened and the approved method of removing bottled socks was with cleansing cream and tissue followed by warm soap and water.

When World War II was over and nylon again became available for stockings, women all over the world - with the same fervor with which Queen Elizabeth gave up cloth stockings in favor of silk - rejected rayon and cotton and even silk, in favor of nylon and almost no silk stockings were being worn in the United States or many other countries.

There is a certain fortuitous irony in the fact that Du Pont which produced Pyralin, a pyroxylin plastic which was sold to many of the makers of plastic darners, contributed to the demise of darners. They put their stocking darner business "out of business" when they invented Nylon.

Just as the materials from which stockings were made changed throughout the ages, so also did the way man "manufactured" stockings. The first fabricated stockings, after man got past the stage of simply wrapping something around his feet and legs, were cut out of fabrics, fitted to the foot and then sewed. This method of constructing stockings was applied to leather, felt, and later to woven material made of vegetable fibers, wool, linen and cotton. These stockings were individually made for each wearer and by the time they were cut, tailored and seamed, they were much treasured.

After the "cutout and sew-together" method of making stockings came the technique of hand knitting. This was a substantial improvement over the previous method because the maker could now, by the process of adding or dropping loops, create well-fitting hosiery. Stockings were knitted with linen, cotton and wool thread, and with the most cherished of all thread, silk.

But in early America, the primary requisite of the early colonists, when it came to stockings, was strength and durability so they eschewed silk in favor of sturdier knitted or cut/sewn wool or linen. Also, leather stockings were still being offered and worn by people involved in arduous work. The Boston Gazette carried the following notice on June 25, 1754:
> "Leather stockings made and sold by Phillip Freeman, at the Blue Glove,
> next to Cornfields in Union Street. Leather Stockings, of different colors,
> viz. black, cloth-colored and yellow, made after the neatest manner."

The hand knitting of stockings was a slow, time consuming and costly process, in spite of the development in later years of knitters guilds and unions. But then in 1589 in England the most important event in the history of knitting took place. According to legend, it came about all for the love of a lady. It seems there was this preacher, the Reverend William Lee who became enamored of, and paid court to, a young English lass. She, either being very industrious or perhaps very shy, spent all of their courting time knitting, ostensibly oblivious to his amorous advances. The good Reverend, resolute in his determination to gain the favorable attention of this reluctant miss, decided that he must devise a device which would enable her to do her knitting faster and thus have time to devote to him. So, goaded by a lovely longing, he did exactly that. In spite of having little technical training, and in the face of forbidding obstacles, he created an apparatus that duplicated the fleet fingers and flying needles of his lady love. He invented the knitting machine!

There is yet another version of what the Reverend Lee's motivation was that prompted him to fabricate his fabulous device. This version has it that Reverend Lee's attentions were rejected by the lovely lassie and so he vowed to get even and put her out of business, by replacing her with a machine.

But the Reverend Lee wouldn't do that, would he? Whether or not Lee's stocking frame enabled him to win the hand of the young lady, or diabolically drove her to the poorhouse, is uncertain even to this day, but the contribution he made to the hosiery industry is acknowledged and acclaimed even to this day.

There was considerable resistance to the knitting machine for some time after its introduction. For one thing, there was a serious attempt by the aristocracy to reserve knitted hosiery, especially knitted silk hosiery, for their own use. The common folks could wear cut-and-sewn stockings of woven kersey or worsted. The wearing of knit stockings was also opposed by some religious sects, such as the Puritans, who considered them to be ostentatious, wasteful and vain, and probably the creation of Beelzebub.

And then there were laws. Even before the advent of the knitting machine, there were laws forbidding servants of the nobility from wearing clothing and stockings with a value of more than two marks. And these laws also applied to the servants' wives and children. There were laws that no servant could wear hose made from fabric that cost more that 20 pence a yard, unless given to him and expressly permitted by his master. Laborers could not wear hose made of material that cost more than 12 pence a yard. There were also laws that forbid anyone except Mayors and Aldermen from wearing silk hose, punishable by fine and imprisonment.

The most bitter resistance came from the hand - knitting craftsmen, who feared the infernal machine would deprive them of their livelihood. There were guilds of hand-knitters in Italy, Germany, France and England, all of whom were panicked at the realization that the knitting machine could put them out of work permanently. At one point the hatred and hostility became so bitter and intemperate that the hand-knitters mounted a series of raids against the factories which used knitting machines, with the purpose of destroying the machines. Unfortunately for them, the crown took a dim view of this activity and had some of them hanged by the neck until dead and some of them shipped off to penal colonies.

And although knitting machines eventually did arrive in America in spite of desperate efforts by England to prevent this, including severe fines and excessive duties, the colonies sought to insure their inventory of fabric and stockings by calling for a certain amount of yarn to be spun by each family, and also be requiring children to attend spinning school. This mandate prevailed until nearly the 1800's.

Incidentally, it is interesting to realize that several of our modern surnames derived from the family's earlier involvement in the production of fabrics and stockings. For example, there is "Weaver" - one whose occupation is the weaving of textiles. "Fuller" was one who made fabric thicker and more compact by moistening and beating or pressing it, and removing grease with fuller's earth. "Walker" was one who stamped on the cloth to shrink and compact it. "Dyer" was one who fixed a color in fabric by soaking in liquid coloring. "Taylor" was one who sewed garments, as in cut/sewn stockings.

This transference of occupation to family name goes back beyond modern names. For example, the name of the noted writer of the *"Canterbury Tales*," Geoffrey Chaucer, derived from the French word "Chausseur" which came to mean stocking. His ancestors were probably involved in the making of stockings.

The styles of stockings have varied all the way from simple strips of material wrapped around the legs or feet to garments which cover practically the entire body, the so- called "body stocking." There were what might be called "socks," which covered just the feet. These would include the Greek "piloi," which were made of felt and pulled on over the foot; the Egyptian knitted anklets which had a separated big toe to accommodate the strap on the sandals; and the Roman "udo" which was cut from woven cloth and fitted to the foot. These may well have been the original "bobby sox."

There were the "wraparounds" which consisted of strips of fabric or leather which were wrapped around the shins and/or the feet. These would include the leg wrappings of the Parthians of 600 B.C.; the Roman "Fasciae" and "tibialae" of 100 B.C.,and the silk leg bindings of Charlemagne in 700 A.D., decorated with jewels. This category of wraparounds could even include the "leggings" of the United Sates Army as late as the 20th century, which were later replaced by canvas or leather "puttees." Then came the cut-and-sewn stockings which covered the foot, ankle and calf; and gradually were extended to cover the thighs and then the hips.

By 300-400 A.D. linen hose that reached above the knee were being worn. In the 1200's, "hoses of cloth" were common. The French called them "Chausses,;" the Germans, "Heuse;" the English, "Hoses." Hoses of cloth eventually extended up to the thighs and were pierced at the top so they could be anchored by cords, called "points," to the short breeches. The points were often decorated with ornaments of precious metals.

From the long hose, "tights" that were worn with the doublet, developed. These were often of brilliant colors, with striking designs and patterns, and in some cases with the two legs of different colors and patterns. They were not unlike the tights worn in women's aerobics classes today; the big difference being that men wore them in those days. They were considered a bit risque by the more prudish members of early society and eventually fell into disfavor and were worn only by servants and court jesters. Still, today's lady might well pay homage to the tights of the 1600's. They were the precursors of panty hose.

In terms of colors and designs, the stockings of yesteryears strikingly surpassed any that came along later, until later in the 20th century when hosieries began producing stockings, panty hose and tights in psychedelic colors with clocks, checks, ribbings and cables. In earlier days, particularly in Medieval times, and especially among the gentry, stockings were colorful and fancy. Even in the period of wraparounds, different colored strips of fabric were used to give a geometric pattern. Leather stockings were made in black, brown, tan, yellow, cloth-colored and other hues. Stockings came in all the colors of the spectrum, including scarlet, red, crimson, pink, purple, blue, green, yellow and multicolored combinations. They were decorated with contrasting colored clocks and embroidery, puffed and slashed with contra-colored fabrics pulled through the cuts, and adorned with gold, silver and precious gems.

Apparently that type of hosiery was not always considered proper formal wear. In the 1700's, some ladies with intellectual pretensions were given the scornful name of "blue stockings," so-called because a noted literary figure showed up at one of their meetings wearing blue, or ordinary, stockings instead of formal wear.

There should be no problem finding the correct hose for any occasion today. The offspring of the hosiery of history are many and varied; anklets, argyles, athletic socks, bobby socks, boot socks, crew socks, dress sheers, full-fashion, garter stockings, golf socks, half hose, knee socks, lisle hose, nylons, panty hose, rayon stockings, sheers, silk stockings, stretch stockings, support hose, sweat socks, tights, tube socks, varsity socks and work socks, to name a few.

Throughout history, stockings have never dictated clothing styles. It has been always been the other way around. Clothing styles dictated stocking styles. Early Asians wore breeches and used leg wrappings to bind their breeches securely around their legs. Roman Catholic priests in 300 A.D. wore knee breeches, so their white stockings reached above the knee. In the middle ages when breeches were short, stockings were long. When breeches were long, stockings were short. When the short skirted doublet became the fashion, tights were born.

As was suggested earlier, tights were the ancestor of panty hose but the concept languished from the 1600's until the 1960's when a slim, diminutive model named "Twiggy" appeared in London in a miniskirt, and it became the rage of fashion. Patently, with the hem that high, stockings had to reach even higher and manufacturers scrambled to meet the demand by pushing an already existing high-waisted hosiery garment and by producing sheer panty hose in 1965. Though the height of hemlines has advanced and retreated over the years since, the ladies' preference for panty hose has not wavered. They have eschewed forever the inconvenience of hooks and snaps and garter belts and the lumpy look.

As it did with tights and panty hose, history tends to repeat itself in other ways. For thousands of years, mankind did not wear stockings at all. It has been reported that even the brilliant Albert Einstein did not relish the wearing of socks. Today, at the end of the 20th century, there are people who have reverted to that ancient status. For them the history of stockings has come full cycle.

Chapter 4

The Ultimate, Infinite Collectibles

One practice that did not survive the cycle very well, is the ritual of darning stockings. While darning is still done occasionally in scattered areas of the world, and there are still a few ladies who darn the holes when their toes go through the ends of their nylons, it has essentially become a lost art and has virtually vanished throughout much of the modern world.

Although the time of the demise of darning is fairly well established, the period when darning began is not. As surely as there were stockings, there were holes in those stockings, and as surely as there were holes, there were repairs made to those holes.

In the Victoria and Albert museum in London, there is a hand-knitted sock which came out of an Egyptian tomb and is believed to have been knitted between 300-400 A.D. This sock had some holes in it which, although technically not "darned," had been patched. While this sock may be the earliest physical evidence of repairing holes in stockings, it is not unreasonable to believe that repairs were being made to stockings before that time.

The reason repairs were made, from early days right up to the 20th century, was always the same - it was easier and less expensive to mend stockings than it was to try to replace them. Mrs. Greek Lady who lived nearly 3000 years ago, couldn't just drop by her convenient neighborhood market and pick up another pair neatly packaged in a plastic egg. So she repaired the ones she had. Later on during the cut/sewn era, when stockings were cut from fabric and tailored individually to fit a person, in essence "custom made," they were too expensive and scarce to discard. So she repaired the ones she had. The same was true of hand knitted hosiery. So she repaired the ones she had. Even after the arrival of the Reverend Lee's amazing machine, the cost of a pair of hose was most traumatic for the common person. So she repaired the ones she had. In the late 1700's, during the Revolutionary War, the price of woven stockings was such that a carpenter had to work more than half a day to buy a pair. And a lady who did housework had to work more than a week! It's no wonder she repaired the ones she had.

So what was is it that finally broke the darning devil's back? In a curious twist of fate, the ultimate event that did in darning was a war! Patently there were other factors involved. The manufacture of hosiery became mechanized, production soared and prices dropped. Man-made fibers were developed which were much stronger and lasted much longer. However, the final straw was World War II. Women were called out of the home and went to work in plants, offices and in the armed services. This opened up new vistas for women and greatly increased the acceptability of women working outside the home.

With the reasonable cost of hosiery and fewer hours for housework, it no longer made sense for most people to darn stockings. That, essentially, was the end of the stocking darner in the modern world, gone the way of the bustle and the button hook - unsung, unmourned and unremembered, but in its heyday the darner served virtually every household with dignity and honor.

The purpose of the darner was simply to hold the fabric taut. And yet, out of perhaps thousands of different darners, there are only two basic designs. One being the type that holds the material smooth by pressing against it, as in the case of the darning egg or the light bulb. The other is the type that tightens the material by stretching it, as would occur by pulling the stocking tightly over the open end of a drinking glass.

All the extensive styles of darners are simply variations of these two basic designs. Over the years, a great many objects have been used as darners. Perhaps the earliest was the hand. Stuck into an article of clothing such as a stocking, either as a fist (the darning egg) or with fingers extended as spreaders (the embroidery hoop), it could produce enough tautness to facilitate darning. Although the hand is the darner of choice even today by some of the people who still darn, most folks, after a few jabs from the needle, got the point that there must be a better way so they turned to such items as bones, rocks, shells, and gourds. There is evidence that immature coconuts were used also, but to what extend could be open to question. After all, coconuts did not grow in many areas, and the South Seas Islanders did not wear stockings.

Mother Nature did indeed get into the darning act in another way. Mr. Charles C. Gale of Glenville, Ohio received a patent on October 4, 1887 for an invention which consists "in an apparatus of darning device of novel construction, by the aid of which the tedious work of darning stockings is not only greatly facilitated, but the stockings or fabrics so mended are neater in appearance and stronger in texture." Mr. Gale stated, ". . .any suitable article may be used as a backing or cushion in connection with this weaving apparatus; but in darning stockings it has been found that practically the least troublesome and best basis for that particular purpose is an ordinary oval of a kidney shaped potato, which is easily obtained and readily replaced when required."

Mr. Gale devoted a considerable amount of his inventive genius to building a better darner. In addition to the above patent, in 1889 he was granted a patent for a darner which incorporated a spiral spring to hold the fabric in position; and in 1890 he patented a darner with a fabric head which gripped the material being darned and offered no resistance to the needle.

Many articles were used as darners including, light bulbs, bottle stoppers, fish net floats, toy tops, roly-polys, pestles, dumbbells, porcelain door knobs, gourds, nest eggs, glass or pottery telegraph line insulators, rubber balls, billiard balls, balls of yarn, bars of soap, and egg cups and drinking glasses which performed in the same manner as the sewing hoop or embroidery hoop. Marbles were also used as darners. These were not the ordinary "commies" (from the word "common," not "Communist") fetched from Juniors marble bag. These were "glassies," some of which were large enough to darn heels and toes of socks, being $3^{1/2}$ inches in diameter. The smaller ones were just the right size to drop into the fingers of a glove as glove darners.

Sometimes a darning session was preempted in favor of a baby feeding session. The nursing bottle was being used as a darner. Many 1800's nursing bottles, blown in glass, were very similar in shape to the glass foot form of darners that came along in the 1900's. Even balls of yarn were used as darners. Jospeh H. Greenleaf of New Haven, Connecticut was granted a patent on February 13, 1866 for an Improvement in Darning-Spools and in his claims for his improved device stated: "The labor of mending or darning stockings is much facilitated by distending the broken parts over a convex surface, and for this purpose it has been quite common to use a ball of yarn. . . "

The term "egg" is certainly most appropriately applied to darners inasmuch as our resourceful predecessors did, in fact, use eggs as darners. They carefully blew out the contents of chicken eggs, duck eggs, goose eggs and turkey eggs and filled the empty shells with plaster to give them additional strength. (There is no record of anyone using ostrich eggs, nor of anyone having feet so large as to require a darner the size of an ostrich egg.) Wisecracks of early day comics not withstanding, there is no evidence that darning eggs were laid by "sewing birds."

There was one small drawback, however to the plaster filled eggs. If dropped or mishandled, the shells would crack and the process of blowing and plastering would have to start all over again. But eventually the smart housewife got a better idea. She would slip out to the chicken coop and borrow a glass nest egg from underneath a protesting hen. When mankind finally got around to making devices specifically for the purpose of darning - instead of appropriating rocks, shells and natural things - he made them in the shape of an egg. How appropriate that was. The egg is the symbol for a new beginning, and restoring a stocking by darning it certainly gives it new life.

Exactly when the first man-made darner was produced is unknown, although there is evidence that from the early days of stockingdom there were ways of mending them. As noted earlier, the 1600 year old sock from the Egyptian tomb had been "patched" rather than "darned" and it is unknown whether or not a darner assisted in this operation.

Some "sewing" tools definitely had been developed long before that time. There were needles in the Paleolithic period, 15,000 to 10,000 B.C., which were of bone, and for those living near water, they were of fish bone. Animal bristles also served as primitive needles. Over 5000 years ago the Egyptians may have had copper needles, which were succeeded by bronze, iron and brass until the 1300's, when steel needles began to be produced.

In an English book from 1893, intended for mothers and ladies engaged in parochial and missionary work, *Needlework, Knitting, Cutting Out* by Elizabeth Rosevear contained this:
"The use of the needle is exceedingly old,
    As in the Sacred Text it is enrol'd
Till the world be quite dissolu'd and past,
    So long at least the needle's use shall last.
A needle though it be but small and slender
    Yet it is both a maker and a mender;
A grave Reformer of old Rents decayed,
    Stops holes and seams and desperate cuts displayed."

Given that Love and Marriage go together, so it was with needles and thimbles. It was in the Stone Age also that stone thimbles made their appearance to facilitate sewing skins together with the bone needles.

Just as stockings developed gradually from Udos, cut-and-sewn and hand-knit all the way to nylons, so stockings darners developed gradually from stones, shells and gourds all the way to the thousands of man-made darners that eventually were created. The darner is not as old as the safety pin which has been around since about 1200 B.C. But it is older than the toothbrush which is about 200 years old, which is not a commentary about the relative importance of darning socks over cleaning teeth. Both might have been accomplished by other means. It is probable that darners were being used in the Middle Ages and particularly after the introduction of hand knitting into Europe where it was being done extensively by the 13th and 14th centuries. According to *The Oxford English Dictionary, Second Edition, 1978* the verb [darn] appears about 1600, and becomes at once quite common; it may be that this particular way of repairing a hole or rent was then introduced.

Some examples of the use of the word include: (1.)"c 1600 Q. Eliz. Househ. Bk. in Househ. Ord. (1790) 294. The Serjant hath for his fee, all the coverpannes, drinking towells, and other linen clothe. . that are darned. (2.) 1603 Holland Plutarch's Mor. 782 (R.) For spinning, weaving, darning and drawing up a rent. (3.) 1611 Cotgr., Rentraire . . to draw, darn, or sow up a rent in a garment. (4.) 1697 Lond. Gaz. No. 3303/4 Breaches darned with Worsted at the Knees. (5.) 1710 Steele Tatler No. 245 P s Four Pair of Silk-Stockings curiously derned. (6.) 1836 Mrs. Carlyle Lett. 1.63. The holes in the stair carpet all darned. (7.) 1881 Besant & Rice Chapl. of Fleet 11 iii (1883) 135. His grey stockings were darned with blue worsted."

There are documents relating to the sale of darners in the late 1600's in the village of Spa in Belgium. Spa is the oldest spring-water health resort in the world and developed an industry of making souvenirs for the stream of visitors. An anonymous author wrote: "From the end of the seventeenth century onwards, Spa produced large dressing cases in lacquer, which contained compartments and boxes of various sizes. According to one contemporary document, these boxes were meant to hold cosmetics, dressing accessories, toothpicks, powder, patches, one ink pot, two small candle holders in turned wood and all the necessary tools for sewing and embroidering. They also made wooden darning eggs decorated with flowers and mottoes."

In the August 6, 1767 issue of the *New York Journal* for the *General Advertiser*, one Charles Shipman, an Ivory and Hardwood Turner of Birmingham, England advertised "Ivory Thimbles and Eggs" among a long list of other turned articles.

In the Shaker Shed at the Shelbourne Museum there is a Shaker mitten darner from the Shaker Village at East Canterbury, New Hampshire, It is signed "GC 1837."

An early United States patent was issued, on November 21, 1865, to Delia E. Holden of Cleveland, Ohio for a Darning Last for Mending Hose which she described this way: "The last is of the flattish oval shape, having only curved surfaces, and one end broader than the other, in order to fit different parts of hose."

The last recorded United States patent for a darner is December 25, 1956. This was issued to Louis H. Campos of New York City for a "Combination Darner Ball and Sewing Kit Holder, " a hollow egg on a handle that held thread, thimble, needles and a small pair of scissors. There were, however, "patching devices" and "sewing machine darners" patented as late as 1979.

Despite the eventual demise of the darner, the fact of the matter is that once mankind got the idea that a darner was a might handy little gadget, everyone wanted to get into the act.

Darners were "man-made," and "woman-made," probably "child made" as well, because it seems that everyone had his/her own idea of what a darner should be, either in design or in appearance. One might conclude that the geniuses of the world, and non- geniuses as well-all applied their inventive minds to creating a better darner. Or at least adding their ideas and refinements to older concepts.

The title of this writing might well be "A Thousand and One Nights With A Thousand and One Darners" because at least that many different types are thought to have existed.

These were called many things, the most common term being "darner." Other names were darning egg, darning ball, darning bell, darning tool, darning device, darning appliance, darning aid, darning spool, darning implement, darning apparatus, darning head, darning block, darning form, darning bulb, darning horn, darning support, darning frame, darning mushroom, darning holder, darning weaver, stocking tree, mender, mending knob, mending aid, mending form, stretcher, expander, supporting device, sewing kit and compendium, not to mention the lighted darners which were illuminable, electric or illuminated. In England, lighted darners were called "torch darners." Some darners were called "crickets." This is possibly from the Old French cricket, one meaning of which is "stick." Or perhaps a diminutive of the Middle Dutch cricke which meant a "stick or staff" and is akin to the English "crutch."

Some darners were called "darning looms" because they functioned somewhat like a weaving loom. They had guides so that the warp stitches could be laid in neatly and evenly spaced. Then a "shedding pin," an elongated metal object, was inserted. This piece, when turned, alternately raised and lowered the warp in the manner that a loom does, permitting the woof to pass over and under the warp threads." Another type of darner had a series of hooks, instead of a shedding pin, which then moved to the right or to the left, raised and lowered the warp threads.

Somewhat similar to the darning loom was the "darning machine" which promised to make quick work of darning. One darning machine, called the Magic Darner was advertised by Sears, Roebuck & Company in 1902 for 16 cents. Although this type of darner was used in the United States, it ostensibly was more popular in England where several were made, including the Tonbat Darning Machine which "makes Darning a Pleasure," and the Speedweve Darner which "Darns 50 Times Faster."

Another name for the darner, although rarely used, was "drawer" derived from the word "draw" which is defined as "to pull tight" or "to stretch tight." That is essentially the function of a darner. The term under which most darners were patented in the United States was "Darning-Last." British patents often used the words "Darning Device."

It seems that almost every language has a word for "darn." The most common term in English is "darn" trailed by "mend." It was also called "cobbling" which is defined as "to mend or patch." Darn probably came from the Middle French darner which is related to the word darn, or a piece torn out of something. Darn is also related to the Middle Dutch dernen and the Old English dernan which means to conceal, and that was the purpose of darning, to conceal, or hide, a hole.

The words for "darn" employed in current usage are often very similar in different countries. For example, "to mend or darn" in modern German is Stopfen; in Swedish, stoppa; and in Norwegian, stoppe. The Spanish word is zurccir; the Portuguese, cerzir; and in Latin it is sarcire. All somewhat similar. The Italians say rammendar, and the Spanish sometimes use the comparable remendar. In France the word is reprise. There is no other word similar to the Hawaiian pahononhono.

The Spanish word for darning egg is huevo de zurcir. The French called sets of small eggs for darning glove fingers, Oeufs and gants, or "eggs for gloves." In Switzerland, among various types of darners used, was the darning ball, called strumpf kugel (stocking ball.) In Sweden the darner was a stoppspannare or darning stretcher.

The names for a darning needle are: German, stopfnadel; Norwegian, stoppenal; French, aiguille a repriser; Italian, ago da rammendare; Spanish, aguja de zurcir.

Sometimes the same words used for "darn" had other meanings. The French reprise also means to recapture or to revive, as a stocking is recaptured or revived by being darned. Reprise in French also means a musical refrain, as it does in English. Another meaning of darn comes from the Middle Dutch dernen which means to stop up a hole in a dyke. The Spanish word zurcir means to concoct lies; and the German word stopfen, means to constipate.

It was not all that long ago that the wearing of gloves by ladies when they were out in public was considered proper etiquette. On ordinary occasions they wore gloves that covered the hand and wrist, and perhaps on more special occasions the arm of the glove would extend to the elbow. But for evening wear, full length gloves, usually white kid leather that reached above the elbows, were considered de riguer. These were slit and buttoned at the wrist and when it was dining time, milady unbuttoned the opening and put her hands through the holes, the better to handle her knife and fork more delicately and to avoid soiling her expensive gloves, inserting the hand part of the glove back into the sleeve part. Needless to say, she took good care of her gloves by darning any holes and resewing the seams.

What was used as a glove darner? Just as the stocking darner was sometimes eschewed in favor of the hand, some ladies shunned the glove darner, preferring to use one of their own fingers. Other glove darning devices were small capsule or egg shaped objects of wood, ivory and occasionally even stone. These were sometimes marketed in sets composed of different sized capsules or eggs for use in different sized glove fingers. Subsequent glove darners, or "darning sticks," took the form of handles with different sized eggs or balls on opposite ends. Some were all wood, some all silver and some ebony eggs on silver handles. Other shapes were small baseball bats and dowel rods with rounded ends. Some also served as needle holders. The list of darners would not be complete without including mitten darners and shapers, garment darners and darning accessories for use with sewing machines.

The makers of glass darners developed their own terminology, not based on the shape or use of their darners, but rather on the circumstances under which they were made. Very few glass companies made darners as part of their regular production line, with the exception of N.A. Amster of Royersford, Pennsylvania; some Czechoslovakian companies; those companies which made the small, mold-blown foot-form darners; and perhaps a few others. Most of the glass darners are one-of-a-kind, made by glass blowers on their own. They were part of a larger group of items called "whimsey: which the glass blowers made to demonstrate their skills, to utilize extra glass, and to give as gifts. In addition to darners, among the more popular whimseys were pipes, canes, walking sticks, pens, rolling pins, chains, horns, cigarette holders, witch balls, swords, daggers and different types of fruit. Also some whimsical items were mass produced, such as hats and shoes, which were used as toothpick and match holders. One of the names given to true whimseys was "End of Day" because many of them were made at the end of a blower's shift. This term is often used today to describe a ball or pear shaped darner that has been "marvered," or rolled, in small pieces of variously colored glass which usually is stretched down the handle. This type of glass is also called "Pick Up Glass" because it picked up the small bits of colored glass, or "Salesman's Sample" on the theory that it was used by the traveling salesman to display the various colors available at his company, although not all whimseys were of multicolored glass. However, the designation that has evolved as the most common generic name for this type of glass is "Spatter Glass," which glass purists reject. Other names for whimseys are "After Hours," "Keepsakes," "Off Shift," "Off Hand" and "Splashed Glass." The English had their own name for whimseys. They called them "Friggers" made by the glassblower when he was "just friggin about."

With the thousands of different darners which may well have been produced, the wonder is that there were so relatively few names for them. While there are many objects called "darners," such as certain long, large-eyed needles, grooved wooden eggs that were used with the metal latch-hook to repair runs in nylon hose, darning machines and sewing machine accessories, the emphasis in this volume will be principally on non-mechanical stocking darners, glove darners and garment darners. Also excluded is another so-called "darner"- the dragonfly.

As indicated earlier, there were "darners" produced for use with sewing machines. These may not have experienced immediate acceptance. There was a certain amount of apprehension among some folks that prolonged use of the treadle sewing machine could be deleterious to one's well-being. Therese de Dillmont in the *Complete Encyclopedia of Needlework* noted: ". . . much has already been said and written on the injurious effects the use of the treadle machine may have on health. We are convinced that, as with many other forms of exercise, far from being harmful, it is beneficial if not indulged in to excess; but if one overtaxes one's strength or overtires oneself, serious consequences many be reproduced in the long run. Two or three hours a day at the machine can do no harm to any person in normal health; and in workrooms injurious effects are no longer to be feared, thanks to the use of electricity." It seems fairly unlikely that "two or three hours a day" on a treadle sewing machine will replace jogging, tennis or aerobics as the preferred path to physical conditioning for the modern homemaker.

Although the most common use for darners was the mending of stockings, gloves and mittens, they were used for repairing many other items such as garments, wristlets, "knicker knees and seats," lace, fancy work, curtains, sheets, linens, towels, knit underwear, sweaters, blue jeans; in fact just about every conceivable kind of garment and fabric. Darners were fashioned from nearly every type of material that could be worked into the proper shape.

The great majority of darners were made of wood including apple, ash, birch, bog oak, burl, cedar, cherry, chestnut, ebony, ebonized wood (a wood stained to resemble ebony called Bois Noirci), fruitwood, hickory, iron wood, mahogany, maple, mesquite, monkey puzzle, oak, pearwood, pine, poplar, redwood, rosewood, sycamore, teak, walnut, lignum vitae ("wood of live," a hard wood from tropical America that is so heavy it does not float in water), and laminated from several different woods. Darners were also made of such metals as brass, aluminum, wire, sheet metal, enamelled ware, lead, steel and tin. Some of the ebony eggs and ivory eggs as well had handles of cloisonne, champleve, gold, silver and mother of pearl. Sometimes the handles were set with semiprecious stones such as amethysts. Sometimes the metal handles served as needle holders, or were shaped into glove darners.

A popular material for darner handles, in the past when it was much more available, was stag horn. In fact, stag horn was popular as handles on a great many things including magnifying glasses, cutlery carving sets, cork screws, hunting knives, pocket knives, dresser sets, letter openers and cheese scoops. Enterprising whittlers even made toy horns from stag horns. The use of stag horn eventually declined due to a steadily decreasing supply - fewer people hunted in order to put food on their tables - and because of the invention in 1868 of pyroxylin, the best known of which was Celluloid, and which manufacturers soon discovered could be shaped in any desired shape including stag horns.

It has been recorded that darners were sometimes covered with cloth, but that would not seem to be very practical, such as the needle would snag in the cloth during the darning process. This may be a reference to those darners which utilized fabric with a long pile as the darning surface. With these darners the pile would tend to keep the fabric being darned from slipping and the needle would glide through the pile without snagging. Later darners, expanding on this nonskid, no-snag concept, utilized what was in effect a short bristled "scrub brush" with plastic bristles, or in one case a "wire brush" such as the English Marvel darner, as the darning surface.

Darners were made from pottery also. One of the better known pottery darners came from a company in California originally called "Itsy Bitsy Pottery," which later changed its name to the Cleminson Pottery. Made beginning in 1941, it is shaped somewhat like a bowling pin, hand-painted with the figure and face of a girl in colors of brown, green, beige, yellow and blue. She has a real ribbon in her hair and written across the lower portion is "DARN IT." She was variously called the "Darning Dolly," Miss Darner," and the "Darning Dodo" and was sold nationwide for about $1.50 each under the name, "CER-AM-EO."

Betty Cleminson, the designer, wrote a poem to go with every item they manufactured. The manufacture of these darners began just prior to the start of World War II when there was great national emphasis on conserving materials and goods of all types as part of the war effort. Given the tenor of the times, the message of Mrs. Cleminson's poem for her darners takes on heightened meaning:
"To mend your ways is dull tis true,
    But Uncle Sam says Make it do
   So stitch in time, else you will rue it
    Let this Darning Dodo help you do it!"

Darners were made of Bakelite, Vulcanite, Celluloid (sometimes called "French Ivory"), cellulose acetate, glass, porcelain, china, paper, papier mache ("chewed paper"),flexible rubber, hard rubber, ivory, walrus ivory, ivorene and horn. They were also made of whale ivory by sailors during their long voyages to and from the whaling grounds. E. Norman Fladerman writes in Scrimshaw and Scrimshanders- Whales and Whalemen: "A carved ivory egg was an especially useful gift. The top unscrews and inside there is room for an ivory thimble, a tiny spool, and an ivory case for pins and needles. Another darning device is of baleen-inlaid ivory and was used for mending the fingers of gloves. The ends are of different sizes to accommodate both large and small fingers." These scrimshaw items were usually made as gifts for spouses and sweethearts, but every sailor's "ditty bag" also contained a darner to take care of his own socks.

The above book chronicles another yarn about the attitude of a sailing ship captain that would have made him most unpopular with the liberated ladies of today. It seems that Captain Thomas Mellen, of the Europa, wrote of his wife in 1871, "she had been sewing continually and got an immense amount of wearing apparel ready for herself and Laura besides knitting three pairs of stockings for me. It is very convenient to have a woman aboard of your ship occasionally if not for nothing more than to mend your stockings, sew on buttons, etc., etc." It is not recorded what Mrs. Mellen had to say about that remark, but Captain Mellen's obvious male chauvinism might well have fetched him a darning of his derriere with a whaling harpoon from the modern housewife of today.

Darners were also made of the most improbable materials. In March of 1938, one Ida B. Peckham of Wethersfield, Connecticut was awarded a patent for darners made of wax or soap. Maintaining that wooden and painted darners would become roughened and chipped and thus damaged fine hosiery, and that darners with hard surfaces such as glass would "damage the point of the needle," she invented darners made of wax or soap. Being soft they would not dull the needle and the surface could be smoothed of scratches simply by rubbing them out. But perhaps the most appealing of all the types of darners are those made of glass including art glass, bottle glass, clear glass, milk glass, ceramic, china and porcelain.

For a tool that had just one primary use, darners came in a remarkable variety of shapes. The most common is the egg or ball shape on a handle. These were seconded closely by the mushroom shapes, particularly those darners which came from the Harz Mountains and the Erz Mountains of Germany and some of those made by the Shakers. It has been suggested that European darners can be identified because their darning heads are mushroom shaped, and that the heads on American darners are egg shaped. There is some validity to this position but there are also a substantial number of exceptions. For example, the darners from the farm regions of northern Germany tended to be mushrooms on a handle, while those from the Bavarian Alps farther south were more likely to be eggs without handles.

    Other examples:
        Solid wooden egg - Switzerland, France and Spain
        Solid wooden ball - Switzerland
        Hollow egg compendium - England, Scotland, Germany, Jerusalem, Switzerland, Austria, Italy
        Glass eggs on handle - Czechoslovakia, France
        Glass door knob shape on handle - Czechoslovakia
        Glass ball on handle - Italy
        Bakelite flattened bee hive - England

Patently, mushrooms and eggs are just two of the numerous forms in which darners were produced. They were shaped like balls, balls on handles, pears, beehives, bells, wheels, shoe trees, rings, dumbbells, bullets, door knobs, ice cream cones, toy tops, feet and light bulbs.

Some darners are "nodders" similar to the nodder dolls whose heads nod back and forth on a spindle. Only these darner nodders are on a spring so that they nod from side to side as well as back and forth. There was a very practical side to this type of darner. The spring enabled one to insert the darner into the stocking more easily. Then there were the glove darners which were shaped like small dumbbells, horse capsules or tapered dowel rods.

Although most stocking darners worked very well in the darning of mittens, some folks utilized "mitten stretchers." These were shaped somewhat like small cricket bats, a narrow paddle with rounded sides and a rounded handle. They were about 12 inches long overall, 3 to 4 inches wide and 1/2 inch thick. There was a detachable section which fitted into the thumb. These devices were also called "mitten shapers" and were used to reform mittens after washing.

Matching the darner to the size of the stocking seemed important to many people who darned. A large darner inserted into a small stocking would stretch it and distort the contour, while a small darner in a large stocking would not stretch it taut enough and would permit puckering. Thus many sizes of darners were made and in some cases, complete sets of several different sizes were offered.

Darners ranged in size from 1/4 inch miniatures to 1/2 inch, for a doll house, to large mushrooms that are 9 inches long, with caps $4^{1/2}$ inches across. These were garment darners, although some similar devices were used as butter or molasses mixers, herb crushers and cabbage pressers. There are some very large glass stocking darners in existence that measure 13 or 14 inches in length. However these were not made to darn socks with. Instead they were the fanciful products of glass blowers' creative talents; pure whimsey.

Some handled darners had hollow handles or hollow caps which could accommodate needles, thimbles and thread. Some held bee's wax. Many of the eggs were hollow and provided space for needles, thimble and up to 5 tiny spools of thread. This type of darner was often called a sewing compendium because the items were, in effect, "in a nut shell." They were also sometimes called etui, or a case for small articles, as needles. The word etui is from the French verb meaning "to lock up" or "to contain." Besides needles, pins and sewing tools, some etuis contained such items as a toothpick, folding ruler, snuff rasp, folding scissors, compass, awl, fork and knife with detachable handle. Another name for a compendium or etui was housewife, defined as "a small kit holding sewing articles, as needles, thread, scissors, etc." In France, they were sometimes called necessaire - and indeed they were a necessity, especially for the traveler. Another device with a French name is the chatelaine which the French also called "menagerie," which translates also to "housewife." The

British designation for these articles, however, carries a connotation that might not be readily acceptable by today's modern homemaker. They called the housewife a "hussy."

In the late 1800's Shreve and Company of San Francisco advertised two housewives. A sterling silver one "engraved or etched" was $9; "plain" $6. A more mundane one in sterling silver was $3.50; in leather, $1.25.

In addition to the darning compendiums containing objects, there is a species of bantam-sized, hollow eggs containing sewing necessities, that are too small to be practical as stocking darners, although they are also called etuis and compendiums. Some were thimble cases.

While the adage has it that the world will beat a path to the door of one who invents a better mousetrap, many of the early resourceful minds must have believed it should have been "a better darner," and the competition to prove "mine is better" was keen. In applying for patents for their darners, many inventors in stating their claims for their own darner's superiority took wide swipes at the shortcomings of other darners.

There was the question of dulling or breaking one's needle. In 1915, Emma M. Olson of Carlton, Oregon patented a "Darning Last" which was a metal "concavo-convex" spoon shaped darner, claiming: "The concavity of the body portion of the last permits of the ready plying of the needle without danger of the needle striking any obstructions or coming in contact with the last, as is usual with the ordinary darning ball or egg."

Then there were the "bristle" advocates. They invented darners with a base of bristles, fibers ,wires or textile fabric with an elongated, stiff pile. In 1884, Charles E. Rames of Chicago, Illinois patented an "Embroidery Cushion," a darner having a "cushion formed of bristles or fiber held in a suitable casing," by means of which "the needle passes freely through the cushion and the work. . ." In 1890, the aforementioned Mr. Charles C. Gale of Glenville, Ohio patented a "Darning Last" featuring a surface of fibers, claiming: "Heretofore it has been generally considered that a smooth hard surface was an essential quality in a darning-last, in order that the point of the needle used in darning should not catch in the material on which the fabric to be darned was supported. I have found, however, that a surface composed of fibers vertically disposed and free at their outer ends, like the bristles of a brush, is much superior to a smooth surface as a support for the fabric being darned, for the reason that such fibers, while fully supporting the fabric to be darned is not lifted from its support, as is the case when a smooth surface is employed, there is no stretching of the fabric darned, which is a point of importance in darning fine linen and similar goods."

Another of the "bristle" advocates was Edwin List Cornell, a salesman and British subject of Middlesex, England who patented a wire-bristled darner on March 10, 1921 which is now known as the "Marvel Darner." Mr. Cornell stated that this darner "has for its object to prevent the fabric from stretching so as to open or enlarge the hole during the process of darning. I attain this end by the employment of a working surface which consists essentially of a plurality of closely grouped spikes or points which are so arranged that when the fabric is placed over or in contact with the working face of the darner it becomes engaged with said spikes thereby preventing any relative movement between it and the darner thereby preventing any enlargement of distortion of the hole in the fabric."

A different sector of non-needle-breaker inventors advocated soft surfaces. John Cunningham of Wilkes-Barre, Pennsylvania in 1918 patented a "Darning Bulb" in which the top half of the bulb "is composed of any soft springy material preferably of rubber sufficiently hard to retain its shape during the darning operation and yet yeildable enough to permit it to conform to the shape of the object being darned." He stated that the rubber portion "will be presented to the article to be darned and the needle used for darning will not have its point broken by contact with a hard object of which the bulbs now in use are constructed and which is a great objection thereto."

Another rubber darner proponent was Belle M. Gingles of Waukesha, Wisconsin who in 1923 patented a "Darning Horn" with a one-piece rubber bulb. She stated: "My invention refers to darning horns or bulbs, and it has for its primary object to provide a simple, economical and durable one piece yieldable bulb, the surface of which is unobstructed, whereby the darning needle, when in use, will not be dulled by coming in contact with a hard surface, and whereby the bulb surface will cushion under pressure of the needle so as to produce a neat and symmetrical darning patch."

In a perhaps incidental comparison to Mr. Cunningham's two-piece bulb, Ms. Gingles claim was:: "it is an essential feature, therefore, that the bulb should be formed with a continuous or uninterrupted surface, for the reason that if a two piece bulb, for example, be produced for darning purposes, a broken joint or bead would necessarily occur at some point intersecting the bulb surface and the thickened bead or joint, thus developed, would defeat the object of the invention for the reason that a needle operation at this thickened point would be obstructed in its passage and either be dulled or broken off, should the point be embedded into said head. Hence in practice, such a possible construction would not perform the functions or accomplish the desired results attained in many improved structure."

Perhaps the most innovative of all the non-needle-breakers was the aforementioned Ms. Ida B. Peckham of Weathersfield, Connecticut. In 1938 she patented the ultimate in non-scratch darners- a darning last made of wax or soap. Her claim was: "One common type of such lasts, as heretofore produced, consists of an egg-shaped form which is usually made of wood and covered with a coating of paint or other similar material This form of last is objectionable for the reason that while used in darning stockings, the needle point will chip the coating and cause hard broken edges to remain on the threads of the stockings as the last is slipped in a thin stocking such as a fine silk, the catching of the threads can very easily damage the stocking to a considerable extent. Another form of a last, which had been heretofore used, consists of a glass form. This has also been found objectionable for the reason that the surface is so hard that it will damage the point of the needle.

"An object of my invention, therefore, . . . is to provide a last which is made of a material that will not catch on the threads of the stockings, when the surface of the last is chipped or scratched by the point of a needle, and which material is also of such a nature that it will not damage the point of the needle. I have found that a last having these advantages can be provided by constructing the same of such material as soap or wax, as either of the said materials is sufficiently soft and plastic at normal temperatures so as not to damage the point of the needle and so that when the surface is chipped, grooved or broken by penetration of the needle, any rough edges or sides of broken sections that may be formed on the surface will not have sufficient rigidity to catch and tear the threads of the stocking. In addition to these advantages, I have found that by constructing my improved last from a soap which is particularly adapted for washing fine stockings, (iron-free aluminum sulphate which has been found from extensive tests, and particularly with silk stockings, to resist runs, rain spots and increase elasticity) the said last may be used as a soap as well as a last, thus offering an advantage for the reason that any scratches which may be formed on the surface thereof will be smoothed off each time the last is used as a soap. Furthermore, such scratches may be easily smoothed off by simply rubbing the last with the hand. This can also be done when the last is made of wax."

One might assume that, if the soap darners were large enough for Father's socks to begin with, after a few launderings they would be the right size for Baby's stockings. Another frequent claim made by inventors was that their darner would not stretch or distort the stocking. For example Mr. George H. Babcock claimed for his hollow Darning Last, (a hinged foot shaped object) patented in 1866, made of papier-mache, hard rubber, thin metal or other suitable material: "As stockings are ordinarily darned the hand is placed inside the stocking to distend it. This causes an unnatural form to be given to the stocking, and as a consequence the darned portion brings an unequal straining upon the adjacent parts when in use, thus causing them to sooner give way and require mending. An ordinary wooden last has been used for this purpose; but its weight is so serious an inconvenience that it is seldom employed. A china egg and small gourds have also been used to distend a stocking while being darned; but their shape is not adapted for the purpose. My improved last holds the portion undergoing the process of darning in its proper form, whereby the above evils are avoided . . ."

Another non-stretch advocate was the previously mentioned Charles Gale who, for his 1890 fiber-surfaced darning last stated: "There is no stretching of the fabric darned, which is a point of importance in darning fine linen and similar goods." Ms. Lizzie D. Carhart of Marion, Iowa also claimed non-distortion properties for her 1890 darning last which consisted of a flat sheet "made of some flexible and elastic material - as, for instance, India-rubber, vulcanized or not" which could be bent to conform to the area being darned. One of her objectives was to " . . . provide a last which will prevent contraction of the stocking or other article in darning when the darn is made. . ."

Another claim to fame made by darner designers for their creations was that they would hold the fabric being worked on. Mary B. Crowninshield of Washington, D.C. created a Darning Last, patented in 1877, which consisted of a ball on a handle with a metal clasp which secured around he handle to hold the material being worked on. She stated: "The difficulty of holding the article to be darned steadily on a ball during the process of darning is well understood among all families; and heretofore, when the work had to be laid aside, the article would necessarily become detached from the ball, to the great hindrance and annoyance of the operator. To overcome these difficulties is the object of my present invention." Nine years later, in 1886, Ms. Crowinshield was issued another patent for a "fabric holder" type darner. The improvements on the later darner over her first patent were "its having two balls, A and B, of different sizes, making it more applicable to all sizes of stockings" and an improved chain and clamp holding device.

George A. Cochran of New York, NY, in 1882, patented a "conoidal form, having a peripheral groove at or near its greatest diameter and a like groove near its vertex, in combination with elastic bands . . . or equivalent means for securing the fabric to said last . . ." In other words a sort of egg shape with grooves at the fat end and the narrow end into which heavy rubber bands fit. He stated, "one of the most trying operations in the process of darning on a last, usually made of some hard polished substance - such as porcelain, hard wood, or glass-and of such form as to readily shift its position by the slightest pressure of the hand, is the holding of the article to be darned in proper position on the last. The darning-lasts now used are devoid of means for connecting the article firmly therewith. Their form is either spherical or ovoidal, hence unstable when enveloped by the article to be darned. To hold the two in proper relation to each other it is necessary to clutch the folds of the article below the last or on the side opposite to that portion of such article intended to be darned, so as to stretch it properly. The small hold the article affords tends to cramp the hand, and if the article and last are both grasped the least movement of the fingers will cause the last either to slip from under the surface to be darned or to be moved so as to destroy the proper relation of the two. Owning to the latter difficulty, it is almost impossible to darn a piece of fabric such as a wristlet or the wristlet of a glove or a piece of lace not sufficiently large enough to enclose the last and provide a good hold. On the other hand, the work cannot be interrupted by temporarily laying it down without disturbing this relation between the article and last, and when resumed and adjustment of the two becomes necessary. The object of my invention is to remedy these disadvantages . . ."

In 1889, Henry T. Cushman of North Bennington, Vermont received a patent for a Stocking Darning Last that incorporated rows of pins on which the fabric was impaled so as to be held in position. Also in 1889, the prolific Mr. Charles C. Gale of Glenville, Ohio, was granted the second of his three patents for a Device for Darning Stockings which incorporated a spiral spring as a "means for holding the darning devices while in operation, and for fastening in position the fabric to be operated upon . . . In the darning of stockings or analogous operations, unless the fabric to be operated upon is stretched or otherwise fastened, there is a tendency in drawing the stitches or darning-thread to contract the opening or to draw and distort the fabric, which cannot be well counteracted when the goods are held by the hand, or fastened merely by pins. I therefore provide a holder made of wood or other suitable light material, of a size to be conveniently held, to which the fabric and darning devices are to be attached in use. Around the edge of the holder a groove is formed, in which a spring, preferably of coiled wire is seated . . ."

Then in 1900, William H. Snyder of Canton Ohio, invented a darner which utilized a "bicycle clip" type retaining band to hold the goods in position. According to Mr. Snyder, "I am aware that heretofore there have been provided darners of a substantially conical form provided with circumferential grooves and elastic rubber bands for retaining the goods in position (see above) but these devices have not been practical, for the reason that the shape was such that it could not be readily held or handled by the operator, the elastic bands would stretch and become lost, and the position of the goods could not be changed while on the last without entirely removing the rubber or elastic band." So the ideas for holding the fabric in place while one darned included elastic bands, pins, springs and clips, each calculated to be the optimum methodology.

Then there was the question of "shape" with each configuration having its own supporters. In 1865, Delia E. Holden of Cleveland, Ohio claimed her Darning Last, made of glass or any other material the surface of which is sufficiently hard and smooth "is of flattish oval shape, having only curved surfaces and one end broader than the other, in order to fit different parts of the hose. "To use this darning-last it is only necessary to drop it into the leg, and its weight will carry it to the place required."

George Cochrane of New York, NY in 1882 said of his egg-shaped darning last, "This form of darning last is most convenient, it having a practically pointed end that adapts it for use in darning small articles of narrow structure such as the toe end of children's stockings while its larger base and curving sides adapt it for use in darning any worn surface."

Along came Alice Anothony of Sterling, Illinois in 1926 with a patent for a "flattened submarine" shaped Darning Last made of hard wood, hard rubber, celluloid, aluminum, hollow enamelled ware or glass. It was available in various sizes and in sets of several sizes. Her claim relative to the shape of her darner was, "The darning forms heretofore most largely used are all, so far as I am aware, of a relatively thick and distinctly rounded or bulbous form, in some cases slightly flattened, but in general approximately more or less closely a globular shape. The curvature of the surface of these darning forms is therefore of such short radius that a darning needle cannot readily be woven in and out in making a darn across a rent of any considerable size, and the short, thick, rounded shape of such a form renders it difficult to handle and hold in place, unless it is provided with a handle, which renders it less manageable and less easily adjustable in the sock. Moreover, unless of unusual and inconvenient size, an approximately globular darning last will readily pass through a rent of large size, and it is therefore impractical as an aid in making a repair of such a hole. In some cases forms having both a leg portion and a foot portion have been proposed, but such forms are altogether inconvenient and unweildy for practical use and great care must be exercised in slipping a stocking over such a form to avoid enlarging the holes because of the bend at the ankle, in addition to which adjustment of the stocking to different positions the form cannot be made."

Many materials were used to make darners and each had it defenders. In 1922, Henry C. Marvin of St. Louis, Missouri patented a glass Darning Implement, although darners had been made of glass for many years. His claims included: "In the use of the usual darners made of wood or other fibrous material, it is found in practice that the darning needle frequently catches in the surface of the darner, interfering with its smooth operation. The surface of the darner is also roughened, which causes it to catch in the material being mended, often pulling out strands or threads. This is a serious objection to the usual forms of darners, particularly where used in mending silks and other fabrics of fine texture and quality. An object of the present invention is to overcome the above objections by providing an article of the character indicated which shall have a highly polished, smooth, hard surface. To this end I provide a darner made of glass or like material . . ." (Taking an opposite position to this premise, were those who claimed that hard surfaced darners, especially glass, were dangerous because the needle slipped too easily across the surface.)

To deal with the problem of inadequate lighting, inventors came up with "lighted darners" powered by batteries or electricity. These darners were sometimes called "darning bulbs," not to be confused with Mr. Cunningham's rubber-headed darner of 1918, which he also called a "Darning Bulb." In 1918, Edna C. Smith of Clifton Forge, Virginia patented a battery-powered Illuminable Darning Last. It was essentially a flashlight with a large ovoid glove of clear glass, milk glass or some transparent substance such as porcelain. The benefits claimed were that it would "greatly facilitate the operation of darning. This will be evident when darning materials having a fine mesh or having a dark color. The usual type of last commonly employed in the household requires two to be on hand. This means that a light colored one and a dark colored one are required for the usual darning purposes so that if the fabric is light colored the dark one is used, while with the dark colored fabric, the light colored last is used. Usually these lasts are either solid or opaque, and the weave or openings to be darned are only seen by reflected light."

Three years later, in 1921, John B. Warren of New York, NY patented his Illuminated Darning Egg which was somewhat similar to Ms. Smith's except that it worked with a battery or with electricity. According to Mr.. Warren; "By means of a device of this character the yarns during the darning of a stocking are brought out very prominently when the lamp is lighted which is of very great convenience especially for people whose eyesight is poor. It has been found in practice that much better work may be accomplished when the illuminated member is used, than could possibly be accomplished when the ordinary darning egg is used. By the use of the device the eyes are greatly relieved and the operator is enabled to darn in an otherwise poor light."

In 1933, Charley Ann Crowley of Nashville, Tennessee patented a Holder for Reknitting Fabrics, which was essentially an electrified egg cup. She stated, "Heretofore a glass or egg cup has been used and over which the fabric is stretched taut by grasping it in the hand and pulling it downward. The present invention consists in the provision of a holder or last which is illuminated from the inside and diffuses a light through a transparency closing the pocket or recess provided in the last for accommodating the illuminating element. In use, the last is used in substantially the same manner as a glass or egg cup is now used, the hose or other fabric to be mended being stretched taut over the last with the portion thereof to be mended being disposed over the smallest end of the last and in this way, the operation of darning will be greatly facilitated."

Thus the battle raged for acceptance by the darning public of that particular virtue each type of darner had.
>Buy me because:
>>"I won't dull your needle."
>>"I won't break your needle."
>>"I won't stretch your stockings."
>>"I'll hold the fabric tightly."
>>"I'm the right shape."
>>"I'm made of hard material."
>>"I'm made of pliable material."
>>"I'm made of soft material."
>>"I won't tire your hand."
>>"I'm light weight."
>>"I won't tire your eyes."
>>"I'm lighted."
>>"I won't snag your material."
>>"Et cetera, et cetera, et cetera."

The first man-made darners were carved or perhaps to be more accurate, whittled out of wood by a thoughtful husband concerned with making the chore of darning somewhat easier for his mate. (But usually managing to control the depth of his concern just short of volunteering to do the darning himself.) Even much later, after the advent of mass-production, primitive, homemade darners still kept showing up. Sometimes to save the 3 cents a store-bought darner might have cost, and sometimes as a birthday present for Mother from a doting child, or as a project in woodworking class at school.

The next tier of darner production after "handmade" was the "cottage-industry" level, often involving all members of the family working together, sometimes on a primitive lathe in their small turnery, to produce many different types of wooden-ware articles which were sold in the surrounding locality.

Eventually mass production and mass distribution took over the field and darners found their way into customers' hands through the notions counters in department stores, dime stores, dry goods stores, and catalogues. In the "mass production" era, wood darners, which were the most common, were manufactured by "turners" who produced a great many items on turning lathes. In some cases, the turner was also the distributor. But sometimes the turner did not distribute the darners, but rather made them or their parts for other companies. In fact, for most turners, darners were only a small part of their production which included handles for tools, cutlery and toys; mallets and gavels; drawer knobs, pulls and handles; spools and spindles; rolling pins, potato mashers, bowls, plates, trays, porringers, ladles, butter molds, herb and vegetable presses, clothespins, toothpicks, buttons and candlesticks; canes, flag sticks, billy clubs; mortars and pestles, and much more.

While the names of the earliest darner manufacturers were not cataloged, some of the later ones were listed in the Thomas Directory under "Darners." The Baker McMillan Company advertised black enamelled stocking darners and glove darners in their catalogue of 1902 and were listed in Thomas Directory form 1905 to 1922. They made high precision wood parts, turnings, shapings, spools, handles, furniture parts, textile shuttles, dowels, pins, rollers and spindles, wood handles for agricultural tools, hand tools, riot sticks and flag poles. They are still in business in Stow, Ohio. Some others and the dates they were listed under "Darners" in the Thomas Directory include:

E.B. Estes & Sons, established in 1847. "The World's Largest Wood Turners" Tool handles, utility handles, knobs, spindles, rolling pins, potato mashers, bowls, ladles, measurers,, butter moulds, clothespins and toothpicks. Now a subsidiary of Saunders Brothers of Westbrook, ME. 1905-1966.

F.S. Gilbert, North Attleboro, MA. 1905-1914.

Gibbs Mfg. Co., Wood and metal embroidery hoops, frames, quilting hoops, outdoor furniture. Still in business in Canton, Ohio. 1907-1924.

Novelty Turning Co., Norway, ME. Knobs, buttons, cord adjusters. 1912-1936.

Stowell-MacGregor Corporation, Dixfield, ME. Spools, and small handles, boxes. 1914-1939.

Stratton Mfg. Co. Stratton, ME. 1914-1940.

Arlington Company, New York, NY. Listed under darners but probably did not actually make them, but rather was a supplier of Pyralin (pyroxylin) to manufacturers. 1916-1922.

E.I. Du Pont de Nemours & Co., supplier of Pyralin. 1917.

American Lumber Products of New York, NY. 1919-1921.

Bogert & Hopper, Huntington, NY. In business since 1874. Listed under "darners" in Thomas 1919-1992, but have not made them since about 1950. Wood specialties of all kinds; turned, shaped or sawed handles; plugs, balls, wheels, pegs, cores, mouldings, flatwork, fancy wooden boxes, locked corner boxes, turned wood boxes, enameled wood handles, wood turnings, and parts. Toy parts, balls, plugs, spindles, finials, knobs, spools, rolls, cork stops, game pieces and toy parts.

Celluloid Company of New York, NY. 1919-1924.

F.W. Peterson of Peterson New York, NY. Also made knobs, buttons, plugs, caps, balls, beads, tool and brush handles. Good white birch wood. 1919-1977.

Care Soo Handle, Sault Ste. Marie, MI 1922.

H.A. Stiles of Boston, MA. Also wooden balls, division of Saunders Brothers, Westbrook, ME. 1921-1957.

The Factories Equipment Co. of Cleveland, OH. 1924-1931.

George E. Goglant of Newport, NH. 1924.

Stephenson Mfg. Co. of South Bend, IN. Beaded and twisted chair spindles. Bent and turned seat sticks, turned and twisted mouldings, steam pump shipping plugs, washing machine turnings, card rack washers, drawer pulls, ornaments and buttons. Baby cab. Handles, screen door, reed chair and novelty turnings, screw hold plugs, crank handles, kitchen cabinet legs, extension table pins and spiral grooved and pointed pins, bushings, gun rods, cane flag sticks, plain and beaded dowels. 1926-1945.

Brown Wood Products, Northfield, IL. Shaped and flat wood work, dowels, handles, turnings plain, polished, lacqured or enameled finishes. 1931.

McLain Wood Products, Phillips, ME. 1931-1940.

Acme Wood Products Company of Cleveland, OH. Handles for cutlery, tools, pulls, children's vehicles. Knobs all sizes and shapes. Wooden toy parts, wheels, balls, beads. Machine cores. Plugs, boxes all sizes, firework turnings. Toy balloon turnings and forms. Dowels: pins - spiral for furniture mfgrs. Rods: plain, spiral and beaded.

Stowell-Macgregor Corporation of Dixifield, ME. 1933.

F.H. Roberts Corp. of Orange, MA. 1934-1935.

Quality Mfg. Co. of Woburn, MA 1935-1940.

Acme Metal Goods Mfg. Co. of Newark, NJ. 1936-1949. Acme Metal Goods Manufacturing Company is a good example of cooperation between turners and distributors of darners. Acme's principle business was the manufacture and distribution of kitchen tools. They produced the metal components, but had the handles and other wooden parts made by wood turners such as Henniker Handle Corporation of Henniker, New Hampshire, and Clement Toy Company and P.C. Carter, both of North Weare, New Hampshire. Acme marketed two types of darners, an "egg" shape on a handle, and a "wheel with bicycle clip" on a handle. The eggs, wheels and handles which were produced by turners, usually of birch wood, were assembled and enameled by Acme. The metal "bicycle clip," which served as a fabric holder on the "wheel" darner, was made by Acme as part of their regular production of metal components for their other products. (The patent for a "bicycle clip" type darner was issued to Wiliam H. Snyder of Canton, Ohio on December 18, 1900.) Conservatively, Acme averaged between 40,000 and 55,000 darners a year which were sold through jobbers and in chain stores such as Woolworth, Kresge, McCrory, and Kress from 1935 through 1965. Although darners may seem to be an odd item for a metal company to market, their "production" (assembling and enameling wood parts with metal parts which they produced for their kitchen tools); and "distribution" (through the same outlets as their kitchen tools) were most compatible and it made excellent business sense.

Cooke-Roberts Corporation of Orange, MA. 1936-1940.

Spors Company of Le Center, MN. 1939-1957. However, they carried a sewing machine darning accessory in their catalogue of 1933.

Boye Needle Company of Chicago, IL 1939-1957. A design patent was issued on July 31, 1936 for their darner.

Victory Manufacturing Company of Chicago, IL. 1944-1949

B.F.D. Company of New York, NY. 1945-1947.

Excel Manufacturing company of Muncie, IN. Metal "Needle Will Not Penetrate." 1947.

Fischer Manufacturing company, Milwaukee, WI. 1947.

Hoffman Lion Mills of Fall River, MA. 1947-1957.

Paragon Manufacturing Company of Ludington, MI. 1949-1966.

Ace Wood Turners of Commack, NY div. of Schutz Brothers. 1964-1975.

Another source of information as to manufacturers of darners comes from the records of patents. For example, the patent for the glass darner issued October 24, 1922 to Henry C. Marvin was assigned to the Owens Bottle company of Toledo, Ohio, a company founded by Edward D. Libbey, Michael J. Owens and others which later became Owens-Illinois. An extensive search of their archives, however, reveals no reference to manufacturing stocking darners.

In May of 1949, Daniel C. Hungerford assigned his patent to the Hungerford Plastics Corporation of new Providence, NJ. This two-color, beehive shaped darner on a glove darner handle was produced in some quantity. Some of the other patented darners which were produced in some volume were the noted Harley Last, patented by Elizabeth G. Harley of Haddonfield, NJ on November 10, 1874; the Atkinson Darner & Mender, patented by George F. Atkinson of San Francisco, California on June 30, 1885; the Armitage Combined Needle-Case and Darning Implement, patented by Herbert G. Armitage of Bay Shore, NY on July 17, 1888; the "Bicycle Clip" darning last, patented by William H. Snyder of Canton, Ohio on December 18, 1900; the Boye Needle company "drop in" darner patented by William A. Davis in 1901; the glass Amster darner patented by Nehemiah A. Amster in 1913; and the "Kit For Sewing Outfits of the Like," a compendium containing thimble, needles and thread patented by Conrad Woge of New York City on July 3, 1928. These are just a very few of what were perhaps thousands of companies all across the country which made darners; from large, mass-production operations to small local or regional shops. United States patent records for 96 years between 1865 and 1961 show that patents for darning aids were granted to people in 23 states, the District of Columbia and 4 other countries. They are Maine, Massachusetts, Vermont, Connecticut, Rhode Island, New Jersey, New York, Maryland, D.C., Virginia, Pennsylvania, Ohio, Tennessee, Wisconsin, Illinois, Michigan, South Dakota, Kansas, Missouri, Montana, New Mexico, Washington, Oregon, and California as well as Canada, England, Italy and Sweden.

However, 5 states accounted for close to one-half of the patents. Illinois and new York led with 14.5% each, Ohio was next with 7.3% and New Jersey and Wisconsin were tied for fourth with 6.3% each. Of 96 patents issued during that period 39, or 40.6%, went to women and 57, or 59.4%, went to men. The decade accounting for the largest number of patents was the 1920's when 17 patents, 17.7% of the total, were issued. The 1910's and the 1930's were tied for the second largest number with 13 patents each, or 13.5% of the total each.

Darners were an essential utensil for every household, and many young ladies, as they began accumulating articles in their hope chests, made sure to include a darner. They were also a favorite gift item, and no bridal shower could be a proper success if the honoree did not receive at least one darner. Sometimes she received a bit of advice along with the gift. At the bridal shower for Mary, who was betrothed to Eddie, she was given a common, plain wooden darner but written on it was this:

"Dear Mary:
When you are married
    And eddie gets cross,
Pick this up
    And show him who's boss.
Good luck to the both of you."

A variation on that theme was discovered in a 1930 autograph book and raises an intriguing speculation as to whether or not this was the same Mary. It reads this:

"Dear Mary:
When you get married
    And your husband gets cross;
Come over to my house
    And eat apple sauce. William"

This has nothing at all to do with stocking darners but which is probably more appropriate advice than whacking him on the head with a darner as the prior version suggests. It was not unusual, at a bridal shower to present a homemade chatelaine to the future mistress of the household. In addition to the usual scissors, keys and purse, many of these chatelaines included a darner attached to a colored ribbon interwoven in to Celluloid rings, with a safety pin to attach it to the belt.

An event that had an explosive effect on the accessibility of silver items to the general public was the discovery of enormous silver lodes in California and Nevada in the 1850's, 1860's and 1870's. Millions of ounces of silver became available and affordable. Manufacturers began using silver in a great number of items including ash trays, hair curlers, hair brushes, noise makers, jewelry, buttons, buckles, sewing equipment and toilet articles. Many of the silver companies made darners with sterling silver handles in the popular patterns of silver tableware and often a bride-to-be received one that matched her tableware, either as a bridal or wedding gift, or sometimes as a promotional gift from the store in which she registered her silver pattern.

Darners were often included as part of silver embellished dresser sets, or what the silver manufacturers called "dresserware." These sets might include a tray, candlesticks, comb, hair brush, clothes brush, mirror, powder box, cologne bottles, hair receiver, nail buffer, cuticle tool, hat pin holder, stickpin holder, tooth brush jar, wax bottle, pin tray, ring tray, nail file, button hook, shoe horn and stocking darner. Darners were also often given at baby showers; generally small sized darners in white, pink or blue. Sometimes they were adorned with colored ribbon and used as decorations on packages.

In addition to using them in the darning of stockings, fertile minds found other uses for the ubiquitous darner. They were used as nut crackers, tack hammers, to play "catch," and as one lady put it, "to hit my brothers with." In an antique shop in New England there was an egg shaped darner on a handle that has been converted to a "Key Keeper" with four hooks around the side of the egg and one hook on the bottom. It was suspended by the handle in a handy spot and the family stashed their keys on it.

One gourd is known to have led a double life. This is a long necked gourd that, having the tip of the neck cut off and pulled with a stopper, served as a powder horn in the War Between The States. Later, having survived the hazards of warfare along with its owner, it was converted to a darner by the soldier's wife.

Some stocking darners were also "hand coolers" -or perhaps some hand coolers were used as stocking darners. Hand coolers were nearly always egg shaped and, while most darners are hollow and comparatively light in weight, hand coolers were made of solid rock or glass; the more effectively to absorb heat. They were made of marble, serpentine, agate, alabaster, onyx and other stones. The purpose of the hand cooler, as the name so adroitly implies, is to cool the hands. Folk lore suggests that they were especially in demand by the young lady of the Victorian era to cool her hands while over-anxiously awaiting a visitation from her beau, or before offering her hand in social situations. Actually, though, there was a much more practical application. Not only were hand coolers used as stocking darners, but also seamstress and needle workers who were involved with white or delicate materials needed to avoid dampness and perspiration on their hands so as not to soil the material. Other methods of controlling the "sweating palms" syndrome were by the use of scented spirits, toilet water or powder. The converse of the hand cooler was the hand warmer. This was generally egg shaped and could be used for darning, however it was often made of pewter which was typically so soft that it did not make the best darner. Its real purpose, after being filled with hot water and placed inside my lady's muff, was to keep her hands warm in blustery winter weather.

While there is no record of salt and pepper shakers being used as darners, even today one might come across salt and pepper shakers made in the shape of stocking darners.

Stocking darners also played an incidental role in the treatment of mentally handicapped persons. At one time darning was a form of therapy for some who were confined or under treatment. It was an activity that kept them stimulated and responsive by giving them "something to do" and a sense of achieving something tangible. The therapists discovered that their patients handled square holes quite well, but that irregular holes caused them apprehension and they did not do as well with them. This would come as no surprise to anyone else who ever darned socks on a regular basis. They, too, had more difficulty with rough, irregular holes. Unfortunately, many holes in stockings tended not to be perfect little punctures.

When it came to men and women in the armed services, a stocking darner was often included in their "ditty bag," a bag in which they carried personal items and sewing articles. As late as World War II, GI's were darning socks rather than risk the discomfort and possible disability caused by a heel or toe protruding through a hole in a sock. The armed services did not award the Purple Heart for blisters or irritated pedal extremities.

The price of a stocking darner varied depending on the type purchased and whether or not it was bought retail or in wholesale lots. If one wanted the plain wooden egg on a handle, the type usually found in most American households, the Montgomery Ward & Company's catalogue No. 53 of 1893 offered the following:

"11498   Egg Darners, white handle, dark mottled
   Each $0.04
   Per dozen 0.42

Two years later in the 1895 Montgomery Ward catalogue No. 57, the price for a single darner remained at 4¢ but the price per dozen dropped dramatically from 42¢ to only 35¢-a very substantial saving of 7¢ a dozen, or nearly 17%. This may well have foreshadowed the beginning of a fierce egg darner war.

The 1896 catalogue of Sears, Roebuck & Company, (Incorporated), Cheapest Supply House on Earth, Chicago matched the Ward prices: "21971. Egg Darners with handle, dark finish.
   Each $0.04
   Per dozen 0.35

The price, for a wooden egg on a handle, held steady in the Sears catalogues for five years, through 1900. But the egg darner price war may have reached its peak in 1901 and 1902 when Sears halved the price and offered this:
   "Egg Darner. No. 18R4994. Egg Darners, with handle, dark finish. Price each ....2¢

However, one year later in 1903, the catalogue of Wm. H. Frear & Co. offered this extraordinary increase: "Darning Balls. 5¢ each." That same year, Butler Brothers, a wholesale house in New York offered darning eggs on handles as follows:
   "Popular shape, black enameled highly polished. 1 doz. in box ....30 cents a Dozen."
   "Cream, mottled in light colors. The most practical for dark hosiery .... 30 cents a Dozen."

Incidentally, when darners were offered by the dozen, as they were in earlier Montgomery Ward and Sears, Roebuck catalogues, they were meant for resale, or perhaps to give to your friends if you wanted to splurge as much as two or three cents for a gift, which was their average cost by the dozen.

The following year, 1904, John Wanamaker of New York jumped into the pricing competition by offering, under Notions and Dressmaker Supplies: "Enameled Egg darners, 3¢." However if you wanted a handle on your "Enameled Egg darner," the price was 4¢ or 5¢.

The same year, Jeremiah Rotherham & Co., Limited of Shoreditch, London, NE offered the "Santa Claus Stocking Darner," an egg-shaped object with a bulbous collar that served as a handle, at 3/11 per dozen. That's three shillings, 11 pence-(in the pre-decimal era when 144 pence equalled one pound.)

In 1905, Sears sold the "Combination Wooden Stocking & Glove Darner. Highly polished, varnished and enameled. This combination darner is made with small end on handle so that it can be used either for darning gloves or stockings,
Price each ....2 cents. Per dozen........ 20 cents. If by mail, postage extra, each, 4cents." Butler Brothers, in 1908, nearly halved their 1903 price per dozen as follows:
"Glove and Stocking Darner. Fills the bill as a 5 cents seller and nets over 100 percent." Black polished. One end for glove, other for stocking. 1 doz. in box. Per dozen, 19¢"

Sears, meanwhile had come up with a new merchandising approach. In 1909 you had "YOUR CHOICE OF ANY ARTICLE ON THIS PAGE FOR 2¢ EACH," and these included 61 different items such as Heavy Iron Breast Strap Slide, a Hatchet Handle, a Milk Skimmer, a Tin Candlestick, a Tin Fruit Jar Filler, a Foot Scraper, 4 Ball Pointed Hair Wavers, a Dozen Lamp Wicks and a "Stocking Darner, 6 inches long, nicely polished." However, to take advantage of this low price, the fine print advised that you must order at least twelve items, so you were really looking at a 24 cent expenditure!

The retail market in wooden egg darners stayed constant in 1910 when the Chicago House Wrecking Company at 25th and Iron Streets in Chicago, in the House Wrecker, a catalog of high grade merchandise sold at wrecking prices, offered this:
"DARNING EGGS, 30-E-238. Excellent stocking and Glove Darning Egg. Made of wood with black enamel finish. The egg-shaped end used for darning stockings and the handle for gloves. Length about 6 inches. Postage .... 3¢, Price ....2¢."

The pricing roller coaster ride continued in 1911 when R.H. Macy & Company of New York promoted "Stocking Darners." Made of hard wood, and with a bright enamel finish; in the favorite egg shape, in either blue or pink; has a strong handle. Price each . . .5 cents Stocking Darner, made and finished as above, without handle.................4 cents. "

Four years later the price for a colored darner remained the same as Macy's 1911 price. The 1915 edition of S.S. Kresge & Company's Kresge Catalogue of the World's Best 5¢ and 10¢ Merchandise from the Original Parcel Post 5 and 10 cent store offered this:
"HARDWOOD DARNING EGGS, 2 for 5¢. BB651-Darning Egg. With handle. Highly polished hardwood. Natural finished or japaned. Weight 3 ounces. Price, 2 for ....5¢
However, if you wanted one in color other than "natural" the price doubled:
"BV6511-Same as above, except finished in hard white enamel. Price each 5¢

The prices seemed to hold steady for a while. In 1918 in the Charles William Stores of New York Your Bargain Book, No. 21 this appeared:
"Stocking Darner. 12V7011. Stocking Darners with enameled finish. Comes in black or white. Please state COLOR desired. Our price, each. .... 5¢

Meanwhile the wholesale price of egg darners on handles had taken a staggering leap from the 19¢ a dozen of 1908. The 1918 issue of the Shure Winner, put out by N. Shure Wholesale Company offered this:
"Handy Darning Egg. No. C6747. Darning Egg, seasoned wood, finely enameled in black lustre finish, fancy turned handle, oval egg; full length 6¼ inch, one dozen in box. Per dozen .... 30¢."

What had become a fairly stabilized retail price of 5¢ for an individual egg on a handle darner jumped by 20% in the 1922 issue of the Montgomery Ward catalogue:
"Darning Egg. Black enameled stocking Darning Egg with handle. Length, about 6 inches. 20 C 4668......... 6¢ Postage, 1¢ extra." or 7¢ total if by mail.

In 1923, the Charles William Stores, possibly disenchanted by trying to pay the rent selling darners for 5¢, came up with a merchandising idea designed to generate some substantial revenue:
"Mending Bouquet. Consists of 12 spools of darning cotton in assorted colors. 1 Thimble, and 1 Darner. Packed complete in a box. Each .... 59¢

Merchandising schemes notwithstanding, the basic price for a wooden darner plus postage edged up. In 1933, the Montgomery Ward Catalogue, The Window to a Great World, offered:

"Darner: Smooth, black enameled finish, easy to work with. Will save you time and trouble. 20 F 4645.
Each ....5¢   Postage ....3¢.

The price, if by mail, had now reached the astronomical figure of 8¢!

Meanwhile, darners other than the commonplace wooden egg on a handle had been making their bids for shares of the darner market. One of them was the mushroom shape as advertised in the Charles William Stores catalogue Your Bargain Book in 1914:

DARNER AND NEEDLE CASE. Imported combination darner and needle holder containing two darning needles. This is a great novelty and is also very useful. With ordinary care it will last indefinitely. Prepaid price ....15¢ each

Another challenger was a variation of the egg-shaped darner. On this darner the "egg" was concave at the top instead of rounded. The handle was a glove darner and needle holder. It was advertised in the catalogue of the Pohlson Galleries of Pawtucket, Rhode Island in the 1930's:

"4499 A New Darner. Curved so that the needle will go easily over place you mend. Can also be used for mending gloves, and the handle contains needles of different sizes ....50¢   (See plate 84.)

Yet another shape of darners was the "Foot-Form," the name given to a darner patented in 1907 which was shaped somewhat like a foot. This wooden darner was featured in the Charles William catalogue of 1914 at 8¢ each. (See plate 74.)

Later there was this in the 1923 catalogue:
Stocking Darner. Foot-Shape ......15¢. Postage ....2¢ extra."

Over time the name "Foot-Form" became the generic name for any darner in that shape. The 1942-3 catalogue from Daniel Low's of Salem, Massachusetts, offered small mold-blown glass foot-form darners as follows:

"KRISTL new streamline darner of clear, smooth glass in lovely green blue, for fine silk hosiery, curved to fit hand. $5^{1/4}$ inch N 224. 3 for $1. Three useful pretty gifts." (See plates 302-306.)

In the competitive world of darners, inventors were constantly trying to create new advantages for their darner. One development was the "fabric holder" darner, one that would keep the material from shifting while being darned. This was achieved either by the design of the darner or by adding holding devices to the darner. In 1903 Butler Brothers advertised this:

"Sure Hold Darning Balls. Combination hose and glove darner with removable hollow handle for needles, $8^{3/8}$ inch long, so constructed that fingers (yours) hold the hose so securely that it cannot slip, thus supplying a missing need. 1 doz. in box, assorted 2 each ebony, green and red, and 6 orange polished finished. 45¢ a dozen."

The 1903 Sears catalogue offered a fabric holder darner, utilizing a "bicycle clip" or "pants guard" as follows:
"Queen Stocking and Glove Darner. Made of black ebonized wood with nickel plated spring to hold stocking or other fabric firmly in place. Does not require to be adjusted until work is completed. Nice for mending curtains and for working the corners in drawn work. Price, each ....8 cents. Per dozen ....75 cents. If by mail, postage extra, 5¢ each. (See plates 181-182.)

By 1905, the 8¢ price had gone down to 7¢ although the price per dozen remained at 75¢. By 1908, Sears was still offering a "bicycle clip" fabric holder darner but no longer calling it the "Queen Darner," although it was the same as the 1903 darner and was advertised the same except that the price was now 9¢.

Concurrently with its acceptance in the United States, this patented darner was working its way around the world. The 1910 catalogue of John Liggle & Co., Ltd. of Singapore featured it this way:
The "QUEEN DARNER." Makes hosiery mending a pleasure. $0.35."

The 1910 Price Wrecker from the Chicago House Wrecking Company also featured a darner with a "bicycle clip" fabric holder, at the same price as the Sears 1908 model:
"30-E-236. Made of Polished Oak, with nickel rim clamp to hold stocking in place. Good for mending any kind of garment, lace curtains, etc. A necessity in every household, and very useful. (Postage 4¢ extra.) Each ....8¢."

In the Sears 1926 catalogue, The Thrift Book of a Nation, this "bicycle clip" darner was featured:
STOCKING DARNER. A very practical stocking darner. Has a metal ring that holds the stocking in place and thereby relieves the strain on the hand. Made of hardwood in natural or black enameled finish. State color. Shipping wt., 4oz. ....11¢."

Another improvement, designed to make darning easier and less tiring on the eyes, was the lighted darner. Featured in Horace Anderson's Giftcraft catalogue Gifts of Distinction 1948 was this:
"DARNLITE. It's an illuminated darning egg to make work more visible. The plastic head of the egg lights up when you turn the red handle, and then even the smallest holes are easy to see. You'll have to think up a better excuse than eyestrain if you don't want to settle down to the family darning when you have a Darnlite. Complete with GE lamp and battery and weighs only two ounces. No. H 4875- $1.00"

After the development of Celluloid in 1869, darners in this material began showing up in the catalogues. The 1904 John Wanamaker catalogue advertised:
"Celluloid darners, in colors, with handle ....25¢"

Not to be outdone by Wanamaker's 25¢ celluloid darner R. H. Macy & Company of New York City in 1909, offered:
"3L 2322 Celluloid egg, stocking darners, with pink, blue or white handles.....................23¢
3L 2323 Celluloid egg, stocking darners, without handles .... 13¢"

Another of the "other types" of darners were those with silver handles and wooden eggs, usually of ebony.

In about 1890, Shreve and Company of San Francisco advertised, among their various silver Sewing Articles, a sterling silver handled darner with a metal collar for $1.75. (See plate 219.)

In 1897, this entry appeared in the Sears catalogue in the section devoted to Gold Headed Canes and sterling silver coat hangers, hat marks, pocket knives, shaving brushes, match safes and garter buckles:
No. 62533. Solid sterling silver mounted hose darner. The ball is made of enameled wood, while the handle is made of solid sterling silver, with raised ornamentation. The handle is detachable, and has a receptacle on the inside for needles. A very desirable present for an elderly lady or anyone who has such work to do. Each, $1.75. Postage, 5¢."

One can only speculate on how many of the prospective buyers appreciated the "old lady" connotation. Incorporating a very substantially lower price differential from their Spring 1897 Catalog, Sears offered this in their Fall 1897 book:
Sterling Silver Stocking Darner. $5^{1/2}$ inches long. Price ....80¢. If by mail, postage extra, 5¢."

The price for this darner remained at 80¢ until the Fall catalog of 1901, when it dropped to 70¢.

Prices for sterling silver handled darners probably bottomed out with this offering in the 1902 Sears catalogue although a different darner that previously offered:
No. 4R6001 Sterling Silver Stocking Darner, $5^{1/2}$ inches long. Price ....50¢. If by mail, postage extra, 5¢."

This darner was offered again in the Spring of 1903 catalogue, but the Fall catalogue of 1903 brought new and larger silver handled darners at higher prices and higher postage:
"Solid Silver Stocking Darner, $6^{1/4}$ inches. Price ....60¢. If by mail, postage extra, 6¢."

In the same catalogue, Sears introduced what may well have been considered by some folks to the excessive extravagance, a "jeweled darner:"
"Solid Silver Stocking Darner, Amethyst set, $6^{1/4}$ inches. Price ....68¢

By 1906, Sears introduced their "Patterns" in sterling silver handles:
"Solid Silver Stocking Darner, Colonial Pattern, $5^{1/2}$ inches long. Price 52cents," and
"Solid Silver Stocking Darner, Rose Pattern, 6 inches long. Price 60¢."

Both of these patterns were offered in the Spring 1907 Catalogue, but in the Fall book, the "Colonial" had been eliminated, with only the "Rose" remaining.

Prices were back up by 1909 when the Eighteenth Annual Illustrated Catalogue and Price List of A.C. Becken Company of Chicago listed:
"Darner and Glove Mender. Polished sterling silver handle, ebony ball. No. 9450 Each ....$.95"

But Sears, Roebuck and Company, "Originators of the Guarantee That Stands the Test in the Scales of Justice," again demonstrated their very favorable pricing in their 1918 catalogue with this:
5N6209. Sterling Silver Handle Darner. Hand hammered effect. Length, 6 inches. Shipping weight about 8 ounces. Price .... 69¢

This darner was of the same pattern as the great many items included in their section on sterling silver objects titled "Toilet Articles," which included mirrors, combs, hair brushes, fingernail buffers and brushes, cosmetic receptacles, nail files, cuticle knives and scissors, shoe horns, button hooks, tooth brushes, hat and bonnet brushes, clothes brushes, letter openers, ink pads, ink blotters, seals and book marks.

Another type of darner that was much in demand in the Victorian era was the glove darner, either all wood, all silver or silver and wood combined.

A late 1800's Shreve and Company catalogue offered two all silver glove darners. One, with a highly decorated repousse handle was priced at $1.25. The other with a somewhat plainer handle was $1.00.

In 1904, John Wanamaker's catalogue had all-wood "Enameled Glove-finger Darners. 5¢."

Calling them by a somewhat different name, the A.C. Becken catalogue of 1909 displayed two combined silver and wood glove darners:
"GLOVE MENDER. Sterling Silver, polished, ebony tips. N. 9448   Each ....$.75.
GLOVE MENDER. Sterling Silver, polished, enameled wood tips. No. 9449   Each ....$.75."

While the great majority of darning was done by hand, there was competition from the manufacturers of darning accessories to be used with sewing machines.

In 1909, Sears offered this:
"Darning Attachment. A most useful article. Will fit any machine. This new darning attachment is very simple and fills a long felt need. With it you can darn stockings, lace curtains, table linens, towels, underwear and many other articles. A great time saver because more and better darning can be done with this attachment than is possible to do by hand. Full and complete instructions for the operation of the attachment sent with each darner.
Darning Attachment and Spring .... 10¢.
Extra Needle Guard Spring. Price each . . . .5¢."

Presenting a somewhat different version of a sewing machine accessory, The Chicago House Wrecking Company's Price Wrecker catalogue of 1910 carried this:
"THE DORCAS DARNER. Machine Stocking Darner only 35¢ Each. 30-E-400. The Dorcas Darner, a new convenience for mending stockings on the sewing machine. The ring is made of white metal and has movable arms that can be easily extended over the stocking which enables one to darn a hole in the stocking on any two-thread sewing machine much neater than it possibly can be done by hand. Directions will be sent with every darner. (Postage extra 5¢.) Each ....35¢

The SPORS Importing Company of Le Center, Minnesota featured this sewing machine darner in their 1933 wholesale catalogue:
"DARN THOSE STOCKINGS Or Anything Else With This New darner. No. N72. Easy to operate, in fact anyone can darn anything with a few minutes practice. Ten times faster and better. Just show a woman a sample of the work it does and your sale is made. BIG MONEY FOR DEMONSTRATORS. An exceptionally good specialty to demonstrate at fairs, picnics, church celebrations, etc. Each darner is packed in an envelope with complete instructions for operating. Weight, each 3 ozs. Suggested selling price, 50¢. Wholesale sample set, 13¢ Dozen lots, 9¢ each. Gross lots, 8¢ each."

In their 1949 catalogue, Sears offered:
"Darning Attachment. Fits all sewing machines. Makes smooth, cross-stitch darning possible on any machine. 6 inch hoop for mending, rips; 3 inch hoop for darning socks. 25¢."

A later Sears catalogue, under Sewing Machine Accessories of Dependable Quality carried this:
"DARNING UNIT. For use on all makes of sewing machines. Darns any kind of clothing, like shirts, underwear, dresses, children's clothes and socks. Hoop is included. After a little practice you can do an expert job. Takes drudgery out of darning. Darning is scarcely noticeable when cross stitched. Use ordinary thread. Not Prepaid. Shpg wt., 4oz.
1 D 6256   Each..39¢."

If a person did not have a sewing machine, there was a separate, hand held "machine"-a dandy little device of tin and wire hooks-to aid in darning, as detailed in the 1899 Sears catalogue:
"A Magic Darner. Mends Your Hosiery in a Hurry. No. 18R4978. The Magic Darner is a machine recently invented and patented for mending hosiery, silk, wool or cotton, all kinds of underwear, napkins, table linens and, in fact, everything in the household that needs darning. One does not have to be an expert needle worker to mend lace curtains and other fine fabrics, the Magic Darner does it for you and saves you nineteen-twentieths of your time. You can take twenty stitches on the machine when you take one the old way. Well worth $2.50. Price, each............16¢ If by mail, postage extra, each, ...5¢."

Also making their contribution to the demise of hand darning were the "patchers" and "menders" that covered a hole instead of reweaving it. One of them was featured in the Lewis & Conger Catalogue of the early 1940's:
"NO MORE DARNING! Give Mend-Sox to any wife who detests the darning core. Mend-Sox neatly repairs a sock or child's stocking in 8 seconds by electrically "vulcanizing" a patch over the hole. With 6 packages of patches in assorted colors. $2.45."

Sears, in their 1944 catalogue, offered an alternative to the electric vulcanizing system, with an iron-on method: "No Darn Quick Menders. For mending men's, women's, and children's hose. Card contains 40 iron-on cotton patches in assorted colors and sizes, with mending knob that aids in perfect, quick repair. Makes hosiery last a lot longer by reinforcing easy-to-wear-out spots. (See plates 156-157.)

Chapter 5

A Pictorial and Value Guide to Darners

Although there is no intent to suggest that the following listings includes all the darners that were produced throughout the world, inasmuch as the number seems almost endless, it is presented as a reasonable representation of that vast variety.

Likewise, the values attached to the darners included in this section are meant to be reasonable representations for the average darner in its category, with the caveat that the value of any specific darner may be affected by other factors such as:

Region. Prices tend to vary from one area to another.

Condition. Is it scarred, scratched, dented, chipped?

Age. Is it old or recent?

Features. Does it have something "extra"?

Rarity. Is it unusual or scarce?

Desirability. How much does it complement your collection?

Origination. Country or area where it was made.

Provenance. Can it be identified by any markings including patent number, trade mark, hall mark, or by design, color, written or oral history or other means?

WOODEN EGGS, BALLS AND PEARS ON WOODEN HANDLES

In the United States, the most common shape for wooden darners was an egg on a handle, although occasionally other forms were produced, such as balls and pears on handles. (More about "mushrooms" later.) Darners are often called "darning eggs" regardless of their shape. While some were natural, unfinished wood, many were stained, varnished, covered with "plastic," enameled in black and other colors, or painted with figures, flowers and designs.

Some wooden darners were "japanned," that is coated with a glossy lacquer or varnish, originally from Japan, which produced a hard finish.

Nearly all wooden darners which were enameled or "plasticized" have a hole, usually in the end of the handle, but sometimes in the top of the head. In those factories where darners were manufactured in quantity, the procedure was to attach them to sharp nails driven through a "coating board" and dip them in a tank containing the desired finish; thus the nail holes that are found in most wooden darners.

The common wooden egg on a handle sold for as little as 2 cents in the late 1800's and even less than that if bought by the dozen.

BLACK

Enameled

P1 Enameled black. 7¹/²". Pear shaped head. Long handle with three incised rings. Well used. $15.00

P2 Enameled black. 7¹/⁴". Pear shaped head. Long handle with small angular knop near head and annulated knop near end of domed handle Soft wood, well used. $15.00

P3 Enameled black. 6¹/⁸". This is the most common shape for darners. Egg on handle with annular knob near egg. Well used. Handle has been used as glove darner. $15.00

P4 Enameled black. 6¹/⁸". Egg on handle with annular knop near egg and annulated knop in middle of handle. Well used. $17.50

P5 Enameled black. 5⁵/⁸". Egg on bulbous handle with knop near egg. Handle has space for needles. Finial missing. $15.00

P6 Enameled black. 4³/⁸". Egg on handle with conical tip. Child size. $12.50

Plate 1

Plate 2

Plate 3

Plate 4

Plate 5

Plate 6

Plasticized

Beginning in the 1890's, processes were developed for providing small wooden articles with a high-gloss finish by dipping them in a pyroxylin-shellac solution. Essentially, coating them with Celluloid. This finish was applied to such items as umbrella handles, canes, pipes, dowels, pincushions, hat racks, towel rings, stocking darners and novelties.

P7	Plasticized black. 6". Egg on thick handle. Note high gloss finish	$17.50
P8	Plasticized black. 6". Flat-top egg on handle with tapered end.	$17.50

Ebony

While most wooden darners were made of such common hard woods as ash, beech, birch, hickory, maple, oak and walnut, some were made of ebony. Ebony is a very hard, black wood that was first imported from the East Indies in the late 16th century. In addition to darners, it was used for boxes, piano keys, cabinets, tables and chairs although it is brittle and very costly.

There was also a "green ebony" which was probably ash, and Bois Noirci or "ebonized wood" which was wood stained black from which furniture was made.

P9	Black ebony. 6¼". Egg on handle with annulated knop and tapered end. Finely turned and very pleasantly tactile.	$22.50
P10	Black ebony. 6¼". Ebony on plasticized hardwood handle with annulated knop.	$20.00

Marbleized

A veined, "marbled" effect was achieved by introducing several different colors into the coating tank. These colors were of such composition that they did not mix, but rater maintained their own individual hues so that when the darners were dipped into them, they produced a finish with multi-colored striae, streaks and blazes. In some cases the colors were added by brush.

P11	Ivory color with red and blue swirls. 5½".	$17.50
P12	Cream color with red and blue swirls. 5½".	$17.50

Plate 7

Plate 8

Plate 9

Plate 10

Plate 11

Plate 12

P13   Cream color with red and blue swirls. 5½". $17.50

P14   Black color with black, brown, ivory, red, blue and white blazes. Unusual treatment of the handle which is one-half black and one-half colored, with hand painted red band separating the two halves. 5¼" $15.00

P15   Cream color with green and red stripes. 5¼". $15.00

P16   Ivory color with blazes of red and green. 5¼". $15.00

P17   Caramel color with blazes of maroon and green. 5½". The enamel had softened at one time and it bears the imprint of the fabric being darned and smudges on the handle. $15.00

P18   Cream color with broad, brushed on blazes of brown, green and yellow. 6" $15.00

P19   Caramel color with brushed on blazes of brown. 6¼". $12.50

P20   Caramel color with faint blue and red striae. 5¾". Shows evidence of much use.
   $12.50

Solid Colors Other Than Black

Darners were made in many different colors but the purpose was more than just decorative. A much more practical reason was to provide contrast and thus ease the darning process. A dark darner was used with a light colored stocking; a light colored darner was used with a dark stocking.

P21   Elongated egg on handle. 6". Plastic coated in luminescent pink. $17.50

Plate 13   Plate 14   Plate 15

Plate 16

Plate 17

Plate 18

Plate 19

Plate 20

Plate 21

P22   Large egg on handle with annulate finial. 6" Egg and handle turned separately. Egg is enameled white (crazed from shrinkage) and the handle is enameled black. $15.00

P23   Small egg on handle with annulate finial. 4⅜". Painted blue, worn through to white base by usage. $12.50

P24   Small egg on handle with annulate finial. 4⅜". Painted green. $12.50

P25   Small egg on handle. 4⅓" Enameled white. $12.50

P26   Small egg on handle. 4⅓". Enameled pink. $12.50

P27   Small egg on handle. 4¼". Enameled white. This darner was part of a homemade chatelaine probably made as a bridal shower gift. Has red silk ribbon rigging interlaced through ten celluloid rings. Additional ribbons suggest that at one time it carried two other implements. $17.50

Figurals

Darners were occasionally decorated with faces and bodies of people. These are sometimes referred to as "The Little People."

P28   Small egg on handle. 4½". The egg is green. The handle is painted in black, white, pink, brown, yellow, and red to depict a "Flapper" girl of the 1920's, with bobbed hair and a yellow ribbon in her hair. Handle is a needle holder. $22.50

P29   Egg with spring "neck" on unfinished handle. 5". Egg is painted with face of a "city slicker" and it wobbles as though he may have spent too much time in the local speakeasy.

This is a form of a "nodder" similar to the nodder dolls whose heads nod back and forth on a spindle. There was a very practical side to this type of darner in that the flexibility of the spring enabled one to insert the darner into the stocking more easily. $25.00

Plate 22

Plate 23

Plate 24

Plate 25

Plate 26

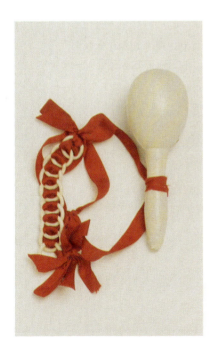

Plate 27

Plate 28

Plate 29

P30   Elongated egg on handle. 6". Birch. This is a flirting "Vamp," with a heart-shaped mouth and coquettish winking eye. $20.00

P31   Egg on handle enameled black. 6". This is a "Mammy" darner with a yellow, red-polka-dotted bandana over her hair. $22.50

Natural Unvarnished Wood

Although many of the unvarnished darners were suitable to be used on most materials, some were made to be sold cheaply as souvenirs and were so rough and unpolished as to pose danger of snagging delicate fabrics.

P32   Elongated egg on handle. 6". Birch. Natural unfinished birch. Stamped "Canada." $20.00

P33   Elongated egg on handle. 5½". Natural unfinished birch. Souvenir of Strawberry Banke, MA. $10.00

P34   Enlongated egg on handle. 6". Natural unfinished birch. Was a bridal shower gift, inscribed in India ink: Dear Mary
               When you are married
                  And Eddie gets cross
               Pick this up
                  And show him who's boss.
               Good luck to the both of you. $25.00

Natural Varnished Wood

P35   Large ball and small ball on short handle with incised rings. 4⅛". Varnished walnut wood. Turned from single block. $22.50

Plate 30

Plate 31

Plate 32

Plate 33

Plate 34

Plate 35

43

P36 Bulbous egg on short handle with annulated knop. 4$^{5/8}$". Varnished hickory wood. Turned from single block. $22.50

P37 Flat-top egg on handle. 6$^{1/4}$". Varnished maple wood. Shows much wear. Handle has been used as a glove darner. $17.50

P38 Small flat-top egg on long handle. 6$^{3/4}$". Varnished maple. Handle has been used as a glove darner. $17.50

P39 Egg on Shaker style handle. 5$^{3/4}$". Varnished maple wood. $20.00

P40 Small egg on handle. 5$^{1/4}$". Nicely grained ash wood. This darner is a virtual duplicate of one located in Miss Phoebe Pyncheon's quarters in the House of Seven Gables in Salem, Massachusetts which was made famous by Nathaniel Hawthorne in 1851. $12.50

P41 Egg on bulbous handle with mushroom knop. 6$^{3/4}$". Turned from one block of mesquite wood. Very heavy. $22.50

P42 Cylindrical egg on thick handle with annular knop. 6$^{5/8}$". Turned from single block of cherry wood. This is a Shaker souvenir from Hancock Shaker Village in Massachusetts.
                                                                                                                      $12.50

P43 Large beehive shape with collar on handle. 6$^{1/2}$". Nicely turned from single block of maple wood. $22.50

P44 Very rare. Large egg on short variegated handle angular knop. This darner is turned from a single block of Lignum Vitae, the Tree of Life, from tropical America. This wood is so extremely heavy that it will not float in water. It was primarily used for bearings, pulleys, blocks, mallets and other articles requiring a tough, durable wood. The weight would make this darner very tiring to use. $32.50

Plate 36

Plate 37

Plate 38

Plate 39

Plate 40

Plate 41

Plate 42

Plate 43

Plate 44

P45   Darning dumbbell. 8". Large ball for large stockings and small ball for small stockings on connecting handle. Each ball and the handle are separate pieces of maple wood.
$22.50

P46   Large darner nicely turned with ball on one end and cone shape on other end of ornate handle. 9". Handle has annulated knop in center, and mushroom knops at each end. Finely turned from one block of maple wood. $32.50

Stained Wood

P47   Egg on handle. 6". Light brown, varnished maple. $15.00

P48   Egg on handle. $6^{1/8}$". Stained brown, varnished birch. $15.00

P49   Egg on handle. $5^{7/8}$". Light brown, varnished maple. Handle has angular knop in middle.
$15.00

P50   Small egg on baluster handle with collar. $4^{5/8}$". Light varnished cherry wood. $15.00

P51   Small flattened pear shape on handle with collar. $4^{1/2}$". Varnished burl wood. $15.00

P52   Small flattened pear shape on handle with cylinder knop. 5". Reddish brown grained redwood burl. Handle is removable but will not hold needles or thimble. $15.00

P53   Egg on short needle holder handle. Finial missing. $5^{3/8}$". Dark stained oak. $15.00

Plate 45

Plate 46

Plate 47

Plate 48

Plate 49

Plate 50

Plate 51

Plate 52

Plate 53

P54   Egg on long handle with angular knop near egg and modified annulated knop at end. $6_{7/8}$". Turned from a single block of maple wood. $17.50

P55   Egg on long handle. $7_{1/4}$". Stained brown and attractively turned from single block of birch wood with large angular knop near egg and proper knop on end of handle.
                                                                                                 $22.50

P56   Egg on long handle. $6_{3/4}$". Stained golden color and attractively turned from single block of maple wood with large angular knop near egg and proper knop in end of handle.
                                                                                                 $22.50

P57   Egg on handle. $5_{3/8}$". Stained very dark brown. The egg on this darner has one flat side so it will not roll when laid down. Marked "Use Merricks Six Cord Thread Hand and Machine for Sewing." This was probably an advertising premium. $25.00

Hollow Eggs on Handles

   The wooden eggs on handles sometimes were hollow and could be opened to serve as containers for thimbles, needles, thread, or beeswax.

P58   Elongated egg on short handle. $6_{1/4}$". Varnished natural birch wood. Egg opens with large space for accessories. $30.00

P59   Egg on handle. $5_{3/4}$". Varnished maple wood. Egg is hollow to accommodate thimble and inside end of handle is slotted to hold paper of needles. $40.00

Plate 54

Plate 55

Plate 56

Plate 57

Plate 58

Plate 59

P60 Egg on handle. 5⅞". Varnished maple wood. Egg contains paper of needles called "Superior Gold Eye Sharps 20 NO 3" from "Fairplay Needle Co." of Germany. The handle is a needle holder containing 3 inch long needles, felt by some to be preferable for darning.

This darner was patented in the United States on July 17, 1888 by Herbert G. Armitage, a subject of the Queen of Great Britain and Ireland, residing at Bay Shore, NY, who assigned one-half interest in the patent to Wilson Pratt of Philadelphia, PA. $55.00

P61 Concave egg on glove darner handle. 5¾". Top of egg unscrews to accommodate thread. Has hole near bottom of egg through which to pull out the thread. Alternatively, could hold thimble or beeswax. Tip of handle unscrews to hold needles in handle.

Original label was gold-printed on black paper inside of top of the egg:

"HARLEYS
COMPLETE DARNER
FOR
DARNING EMBROIDERING
AND
GLOVE MENDING"

Marked: "Pat. Nov. 10, 74"

This is one of the most sought-after darners, the famous "Harley Darner." It was patented on November 10, 1874 by Elizabeth G. Harley of Haddonfield, New Jersey and introduced at the Women's Pavilion at the 1876 Centennial Exposition in Philadelphia. Her patent application stated: "The object of my invention is to provide a simple and convenient device for use in the operation of darning, embroidering, or the like, which end shall embody in its construction means for supporting the material worked upon, and receptacles for the thread and needles; to which end my improvement consists in combining, with a hollow stretcher having a concave surface for holding the work, and a receptacle for containing a ball of thread, a hollow handle, which serves as a needle receptacle . . . . ."

This darner was called "The Complete Darner" in the book "The Centennial Exposition" by J.S. Ingram published in 1876. $75.00

However, Mrs. Harley was not the first to put a hole in a darner from which to draw out the thread. Mr. Orsamus C. Glynn of New Haven, Connecticut patented one 9 months earlier on February 24, 1874. He stated that it has a "Perforation through which the yarn is drawn out as required."

P62 Also a Harley darner of different wood that P61. Displayed open to show construction.
$75.00

Plate 60

Plate 61

Plate 62

Primitives

    The word "primitive" has different meanings. One meaning is of "times long ago"; another meaning is "simple" or made in an old-fashioned style. Many primitive darners were handmade; carved out of available wood and were one of a kind. Others were produced on turning lathes, which date from the ancient hand-powered lathes of the Egyptians, Greeks and Romans (although they probably did not make darners) to later electrical powered lathes on which school boys turned out darners in woodcraft shop. It is the "style" rather than the "age" which identifies the primitive darner.

P63   Egg on bulbous handle. Varnished white oak. Although oak is a very hard wood, the open graining of this darner would tend to snag the needle in darning. Probably made in wood shop. $6^{1/4}$". $15.00

P64   Small ball on handle with smaller ball on other end. Turned from one piece of soft wood which is not well suited for a darner. Deeply scarred by much usage. $5^{1/2}$". $22.00

P65   Spheroidal ball on bulbous handle with six incised rings. Turned from single piece of wood. Made of maple which is very hard and splits fairly easily. Split on this darner runs from end of handle into the ball. A small portion of one side is flattened, either intentionally or accidentally, which provides a "non-roll" feature which was designed into some other darners. $5^{1/4}$". $15.00

P66   Cylinder shaped head on bulbous handle. Crudely made from single piece of cherry wood. Head is split. 6" $15.00

P67   Large egg on short, stubby handle with three incised rings at end of handle. Nicely turned from single piece of walnut. $4^{3/4}$". $20.00

P68   Large rounded cylinder on handle, hand-carved from single block of red oak. 8". $20.00

Plate 63

Plate 64

Plate 65

Plate 66

Plate 67

Plate 68

P69   Large egg and small egg on handle turned from single piece of hickory. 8" $50.00

P70   Large egg for toes and ball for heels. Turned from single piece of birch lacquered red. This has been called a "bastard" darner in the sense that it is irregular or unusual in form, size or proportion. As Gertrude Whiting states in *Old Time Tools and Toys of Needlework:* "From Honolulu sailed in early days the good ship Morning Star. Children in the homeland, whence had come these all-enduring missionaries, contributed ten cents a head toward the building of the brig. She was to carry the Gospel to the Micronesian islands. After ten years the boat was nearly worn out and her name was changed to the Harriet Newell; she sailed and never again was heard from; In '66 went forth a second Morning Star. She broadsided a reef. So a third Morning Star was launched to Mokil, Ponape, Pingelap, the Mortlock Islands and Ruk. Number three was also reefed. From her worm-eaten wood was made the big bastard darning ball here shown. The Chief Mate-C.S. Lewis block of historic wood and whittled the ball for this wife, Lucy Wetmore." It currently belongs to the Children and Cousins' Society, Hawaii.

The darner shown here is the exact shape of the Morning Star darner, except it is painted red. $6^{3/4}$". $25.00

P71   Large egg on handle with squared knop at end of handle. Turned from solid piece of bird's eye maple. Lightly varnished. $22.00

P72   Small mushroom on one end of "dowel" handle with beehive at other end. Stained dark and lightly varnished. $22.00

WOODEN FOOT FORMS

The term "Foot Form" was originally a registered trade mark for a specific wooden darner, the front end of which was shaped in such a way as to fit into the toe of a sock. The term evolved into the generic word for any darner wood, glass, plastic or other material, made in this shape.

Natural Foot Forms

P73   Standard foot form. Stained and lightly varnished birch wood. Marked: "FOOT FORM PAT. NOV. 1907." A design patent for this darner was issued to Emily Waitee Thayer of Saxton's River, Vermont on November 19, 1907. This darner was advertised for 8 cents in 1914, and 15 cents in 1923. $5^{1/2}$" long, $2^{9/16}$"" wide' and $1^{9/16}$" thick. $15.00

P74   Standard foot form. Natural birch wood. Marked: "FOOT FORM Patented." This is a later version of P73 and demonstrates the changing shape of this darner. It is thinner in the toe with a somewhat longer handle. $5^{3/8}$" long, long; $2^{3/8}$" wide; and $1^{1/2}$" thick. $15.00

Plate 69

Plate 70

Plate 71

Plate 72

Plate 73

Plate 74

Enamelled Foot Forms

P75   Standard foot form enameled light blue color. Has nail hole in end of handle from being attached to a dipping board. 5 5/8" long; 2 1/2" wide; and 1 9/16" thick. $17.50

P76   Standard foot form enameled ivory color. 5 1/2" long; 2 3/8" wide; 1 7/16" thick. $17.50

Handled Foot Forms

P77   Small elliptical varnished birch foot form on an enameled handle. Marked: "Pat. Pend."

    $15.00

Combination Foot Forms

P78   Curved elliptical foot form on a dowel handle with mushroom cap at other end. Lightly varnished natural color wood. 6 1/2" long. Origin is obscure although it has been postulated by some to be a "Shaker double darner."

This darner appears to be an earlier version of a darner patented on December 8, 1932 by Anna K. Frazier of Leavenworth, Kansas. She stated ". . . one object of the invention is to provide a last of such formation that when it is placed within a stocking and particularly the toe portion of the stocking, it will not cause the stocking to be distorted by stretching and not fit properly upon a person's foot when worn." $30.00

P79   Side view of P78

Plate 75

Plate 76

Plate 77

Plate 78

Plate 79

57

WOODEN DARNERS WITH GLOVE DARNER HANDLES

P80   Egg with glove darner handle. Varnished dark wood. Space in handle for needles (stuck in spongy reed) and thimble.

Marked "Atkinson Darner
        U.S. Pat. June 30, 85"

This darner was patented by George F. Atkinson of San Francisco, California, patent #320,995 dated June 30, 1885. $6^{1/2}$".

The primary patent claim was that the egg has a "tapering socket for the purpose of securing a perfect joint without a shoulder upon the mender not effected by shrinkage of the wood, and to secure a needle and thimble holder, the thimble serving as a cap for the needle-holder to keep the needles from falling out when the mender is withdrawn from the stretcher . . ."

In other words, the handle fit snugly into the egg without screwing it on. $30.00

P81   This is another version of the Atkinson darner, marked on the egg "Pat. June 30, 1885." It is different from P80, which has the egg and handle both made from the same type of wood, in that it has an egg made of a different, contrasting light wood. $6^{1/2}$". $25.00

P82   Egg on fairly thick glove darner handle with space in handle for needles and thimble. Made of varnished red wood. Side of egg is marked "California Big Tree." Partial label indicates Santa Cruz County in California. $6^{7/8}$" $30.00

P83   Egg on glove darner handle with space in handle for needles and thimble. Made of varnished red wood. Marked around the top of the egg "California Big Tree." Partial label indicates Santa Cruz County in California. $6^{7/8}$" $30.00

P82 and P83 are nearly identical to the Atkinson darner and may be later models of it, although there is some slight variation in size and shape.

Plate 80

Plate 81

Plate 82

Plate 83

59

P84 Concave bell shape on glove darner handle which is also a needle holder. Varnished maple. This darner was advertised in the early 1930's as "Curved so that the needle will go easily over place you mend. Can also be used for mending gloves, and the handle contains needles of different sizes . . . 50 cents." 5". $17.50

P85 Concave bell shape on glove darner handle. Enameled black. 5½". $15.00

P86 Semi cone with glove darner handle. Varnished maple, turned from one piece of wood. 6½".
        Stamped:
        USED FOR
        STOCKING MS GLOVES
        ALL WOOLEN ARTICLES
        DARNING APPLIANCE

(MS-S is superimposed on M) $25.00

COMPOSITES, TUNBRIDGEWARE, STICKWARE

The common trait that runs through composite darners is that they are made from several different woods of contrasting colors that were glued together before being turned. The two types of composites are "end grain" where the patterns are formed by the ends of the sticks, and "stickwork" where the predominant grain runs lengthwise.

The most noted of the end grain items, called Tunbridge Ware, came from Tunbridge Wells, Kent, England beginning in the 1700's. This type of work was also called Tunbridge Mosaic and Wood Mosaic. In the 1800's "stickware" made its appearance. Stickware was also made in other areas, notably Germany and Switzerland. Tunbridge probably produced more sewing tools than all the other souvenir ware industries, and in a much greater variety. The last makers of Tunbridge Ware disappeared in the 1920's.

P87 Large Tunbridge end-grain mushroom on bulbous handle. Laminated with 83 pieces of wood including dark brown, light brown, gray and dyed red and green. Woods used in Tubridgeware include oak, hickory, maple, mahogany, ebony, holly, cherry, plum, yew and sycamore. Ca 1880. 5¼" $140.00

P88 Top view of P87

P89 Quasi dumbbell shape stickware darner. Nine alternating layers of 1/2" walnut and 1/8" maple wood. 6¾" long. $45.00

Plate 84

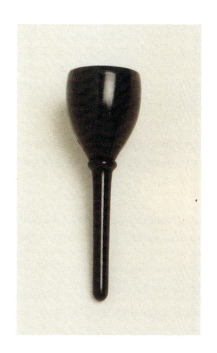

Plate 85

Plate 86

Plate 87

Plate 88

Plate 89

P90   Egg on handle with angular knop at bottom of egg and ball knop at end of handle. Comprised of 5 pieces of wood. Maple wood with 4 black cherry "spots" around the egg. Nicely turned. 7".

Probably "Prison Art." There is a candlestick in Vergennes, Vermont that is identical in wood and design that is labeled "Made by Inmate of the State Prison." $57.00

P91   Egg on glove darner handle. Comprised of 13 pieces of maple and walnut wood. Extremely well executed. $7^{5/8}$" long. $65.00

P92   Classic "stickware" egg on handle. Egg is comprised of 34 square alternating sticks of black walnut and maple. Handle is painted green with pink and white beaded flowers and an angular knop on the end. $6^{3/8}$" long. $65.00

P93   Small ball on handle with mushroom knop at top and ball knop at bottom. Ball is separate, comprised of 70 small rectangular sticks alternating light and dark wood. Handle is single piece of walnut. $5^{7/8}$" long. $30.00

P94   Stickware egg. Comprised of 25 alternating 1/2" square sticks of black cherry and maple in "checkerboard" pattern. From Switzerland. $3^{1/2}$" $40.00

P95   Stickware ball. Comprised of 32 3/8" square sticks of maple and walnut wood in "checkerboard pattern." From Switzerland. $2^{1/8}$" diameter. $30.00

P96   Large quais dumbell with ball on one end and egg shape on the other end. Unusual stickware pattern composed of 31 1/4" square sticks and 10 1/8" laminae. Maple and walnut. 9" $120.00

Plate 90

Plate 91

Plate 92

Plate 93

Plate 94

Plate 95

Plate 96

WOODEN MUSHROOMS AND BEEHIVES

Second in popularity, in America, to the egg shaped darners were the mushrooms; although the mushroom was a predominant shape in most of Europe. Not only are they a utilitarian shape for darning, but also because the mushroom was a totem of prehistoric significance in many European countries such as Germany, Austria, Poland, Latvia, Russia and others. The poisonous Amanita muscaria, or "Fly Agaric," because soaked in milk or a bit of honey it was a fly killer, was used in controlled amounts by neolithic shamans to induce hallucinogenic visions. The people believed they could reach the gods only through the shamans and since the mushroom was essential to this activity it took on compelling religious significance. That import has carried over even today where in many places the mushroom is a symbol for "good luck."

Natural, Unvarnished Wood Mushrooms

P97   Lathe turned mushroom on handle with beehive knop. Cap and handle turned separately. Maple 4¾". $25.00

P98   Small mushroom on needle holder handle. Maple. 4½" $25.00

P99   Small mushroom on needle holder handle. Maple. 4¼" $20.00

P100 Small bulbous mushroom on handle with two annular grooves. Turned from single piece of wood. 4¼". $20.00

P101 Small mushroom on handle. Cap and handle turned separately. Birch wood. 3½".
                                                                                $20.00

P102 Small beehive on handle with pointed final. 5" $25.00

Plate 97

Plate 98

Plate 99

Plate 100

Plate 101

Plate 102

P103 Small beehive on needle holder handle. Unfinished birch wood. 4 1/2". This darner belonged to Miss Sallie High Thomson of Union County, South Carolina who was born in 1857 and died in 1952. She grew up on a farm and moved to Herndon Terrace with her brother, William Elias Thomson, when he married. She took care of their mother until she died, then lived on there for the rest of her lfe in complete charge of domestic arrangements; the servants, meals, chickens, cow, vegetable gardens. She read the Bible every night. She didn't laugh out loud, but had a wonderful sense of humor and smiled. She was called "Angel," "Auntie," and "Miss Sallie"

$40.00

Natural, Varnished Wood Mushrooms

P104 Mushroom on threaded needle holder handle with turned finial. Maple. 4 3/8". $25.00

P105 Thin mushroom cap on slender handle ending in a thimble shaped glove darner. From Denmark. 4 3/8". $30.00

P106 Small mushroom on handle which is laminated from four pieces of wood. Beech wood. 3 3/4". $20.00

P107 Small mushroom on needle holder handle. Finial is missing. 3 3/4". $15.00

P108 Mushroom on handle with two grooves and bun finial. Maple wood. 5 1/4" $15.00

Stained Wood Mushrooms

P109 Mushroom on handle with thimble and needle holder handle and plastic stopper. Stained coco bolo wood. This is a new darner from the woodcarving center of Grindelwald, Switzerland. 4 1/2". $25.00

Plate 103

Plate 104

Plate 105

Plate 106

Plate 107

Plate 108

Plate 109

P110   Mushroom on cylindrical needleholder handle with metal collar around base of cap. Stained brown. Imprinted "FRANCIS SMITH", the name of the owner, and "CUMBERLAND PENCIL CO. KESWICK." From the "Lake District in northern England, a tourist area famous for its scenery. Many of the pencils Cumberland made were fine colored pencils for artists. $50.00

P111   Mushroom on needle holder handle with angular knops ball finial. Varnish red pine wood. Imprinted "LILY FEENEY." From England. 5". $40.00

P112   (a) Small "wheel" grooved on the bottom, on short grooved handle. Walnut wood. $2^{1/4}$"
    $20.00

    (b) Very small "wheel" grooved on bottom, on short grooved handle. Walnut wood. These are companion pieces. $1^{3/4}$" $15.00

P113   (a) Very large mushroom on handle. Garment darner. Natural sugar maple, lightly varnished. Measures $8^{1/2}$" tall with $4^{3/4}$" cap. Somewhat similar devices were "herb crushers," "cabbage presses," "butter workers" or "mixers," but they would not be varnished.
    $50.00

    (b) Very small mushroom on needle holder handle. Golden maple wood. $2^{1/4}$".
    $15.00

Beehives

P114   Beehive on stubby handle. Varnished beech wood. $4^{1/8}$". $17.50

P115   Beehive on stubby handle. Painted white and hand decorated with two stockings hanging on a clothes line. $3^{7/8}$" $20.00

Plate 110

Plate 111

Plate 112

Plate 113

Plate 114

Plate 115

Painted Wood Mushrooms - Swirls

P116   Mushroom on handle. Painted in swirls of red, green, and tan. Handle contains compendium consisting of two spools, needle holder, glove darner and space for thimble. Impressed "Germany." 4¾". $35.00

P117   Mushroom on handle with angular knop. Enameled with swirls of silver and blue. 5". $30.00

Painted Wood Mushrooms - Solid Colors

P118   Nicely constructed green mushroom cap in yellow glove darner handle. Very unusual for mushrooms to have glove darner handles. $25.00

Painted Wood Mushrooms - Red Caps

P119   Mushroom on handle. The mushroom is called "Pilz" in German. Cap painted red and is split. Handle is varnished ash. 4½". $15.00

P120   Mushroom on handle. Well worn cap painted red. Handle is varnished oak. $17.50

P121   (a) Mushroom on handle. Cap painted red with white dots. Handle is varnished. Made of beech wood. 4¼" $25.00

(b) Miniature mushroom on handle for doll house. Cap painted red with yellow dots. 1¾" overall. $15.00

A mushroom with red cap which is dotted with white or light colored spots is typical of the darners made in the farm regions in the northern part of Germany in Erz Gebirge (the Erz chain of mountains) and in the Harz mountains, generally in the cold winter months from the ready supply of beech wood. The Harz mountains, situated in the heart of Germany, are ideal for hiking and the vigilant hiker may well see trolls and witches said to be still dancing around the Brocken, the highest peak in the area.

Plate 116

Plate 117

Plate 118

Plate 119

Plate 120

Plate 121

P122 Mushroom on handle. Well worn cap is painted red with white dots. Handle is European walnut with needle holder and finial. Handle is inscribed "Hilsen Fra Molde" or "Greetings from Molde." Molde is a town and fiord about 150 miles northwest of Oslo, Norway near the Atlantic Ocean. This darner was owned by Harriet Jahnsen who was born in 1896 in Moss, Norway. 3¾". $30.00

P123 Small mushroom on bulbous handle. Cap painted red with white dots. Needle holder handle painted white. 3¼". $25.00

P124 Small mushroom on bulbous handle. Cap painted red. Thimble case handle. 2¼". $22.50

P125 Thick mushroom on needle holder handle. Cap is stained brown with lighter tan spots. Handle is enameled black with engraved "raindrops" down its length. From Denmark. 4¼". $30.00

Painted Wood Mushroom - Floral & Garden Decorations

P126 Mushroom on needle holder handle. Cap is painted with flowers in blue, green, yellow and red. Grooves around rim of cap and on handle painted brown. Labelled "Made in Czechoslovakia." 4½". $30.00

P127 Mushroom on handle. Cap hand painted with pink flower, green leaves and black and white center. 4½" $20.00

P128 Mushroom on screw-on needle holder handle with annulated finial. Cap is hand painted in green, yellow, purple, blue, pink, tan and white, picturing a thatched roof cottage surrounded by a tree and garden. Handle is yellow. 4½". $30.00

P129 Mushroom on handle. Natural wood color painted red with stylized flowered on cap in red and black. Also underside of cap and handle decorated in red and black. Ukrainian, ca 1850. 4¼" $20.00

Plate 122   Plate 123

Plate 124

Plate 125

Plate 126

Plate 127

Plate 128

Plate 129

P130   Primitive pseudo mushroom on handle. Cap is decorated with concentric circles hand painted in red, black and brown. From England. 3¼" $15.00

Mauchline Wood Mushrooms

Mauchline is a Scottish ware developed in the 1820's in the Scottish town of Mauchline in Ayrshire. Originally the pictures were drawn directly on the wood with India ink. By the 1830's the wood items were decorated with transferred engravings and this type is referred to as "transferware." Mauchline "Fernware" was made by holding leaves of ferns against the wood and spray painting them leaving the outline of the leaf on the wood, as was "Seaweed" and "Floral" ware. Another type of Mauchline features Scotch plaids. It was called "Scotch goods" and "Clan tartan wood work" until it became known as "Tartanware" and was included in the generic term "Mauchline." Tartanware was sometimes marked "Caledonia" which is the Roman name for Scotland, or with the name of the tartan, such as "Campbell" or "Stuart."

P131   Mushroom on bulbous screw-on needle holder handle. Varnished maple inlaid with pear wood. The cap has a Mauchline picture depicting a shoreline and the wording "Ostseebad Niendorf" which translates to "East Seaside Resort Niendorf" or "Channel Spa at Niendorf." German, ca 1860-1885. 4½". $50.00

P132   Mushroom with screw on needle holder handle with finial. White maple. The Mauchline picture is "metamorphic," one meaning of which is "a change in form, structure, or substance by, or as if by, witchcraft, transformation." Or "noticeable or complete change of character, appearance, circumstances, etc."The picture shows a couple. Held one way it reads "Braustand" or "Fiancees" and shows them in their fine clothes while courting. (Enlarged to show detail).

P133   Turned the other side up and the caption is "Chestand" or Married" and the same picture is transformed to show them, after they are married, in their night caps. 4". (Enlarged to show detail). $100.00
The "Before and After" design was done in several variations. Boston and Sandwich Glass Company and New England Glass Company of Cambridge, Massachusetts used them on some of their cup plates. One was the "Wedding Day" pattern, made ca. 1840-1860. If the "Wedding Day" inscription is upright the faces are smiling. If "Three Weeks After" is up right, the faces are frowning.

P134   Mushroom on handle. Cap is "Tartan Ware" and labeled "Stuart." Handle and underside of cap are enameled black. Tartan ware is a form of Mauchline. 4¼" $140.00

Wood Mushrooms with Printed Messages

P135   Thin maple mushroom with collar on elaborate black walnut ball handle. Cap has groove around edge, ostensibly for elastic band to hold fabric. 2¾". $35.00
Carries the following advertisement:

>Men's Cardigan Jackets
>for good and reliable
>HOSIERY go to
>GREENWOODS
>10 tr??? Street
>K?BEY STAFF
>A Specialty

Plate 130

Plate 131

Plate 132

Plate 133

Plate 134

Plate 135

P136 Mushroom on handle. Varnished natural maple. Cap is hand decorated with stylized flower and inscribed in German. Translated, it says essentially:
"It will be the biggest love ever
If you will daily darn my socks."
This is a new souvenir, called a "stopfliz" (stopf = darn; pilz= mushroom) purchased at the Oberlander Heimatwerk (Highland Native Art Shop) in Spiez, Switzerland. 5"
$50.00

P137 Coal black mushroom on handle. Intricately carved with shamrocks and a harp. This darner is made of bog oak. The color is the result of coming from the peat bogs in Ireland. Purchased in Camden Passage, London, England. 3 1/4". $60.00

SOLID WOODEN EGGS, BALLS, CAPSULES, CONES, AND PESTLES

It is fairly common speculation that early man-made darners were in the shape of eggs without handles, although no record has been found to substantiate that belief. However, there is no question that the simple egg darner was widely used. Certainly it is appropriate inasmuch as the egg has come to be recognized as the symbol for renewal, which is what happens when a darning egg helps "renew" a stocking.

Colored/Decorated

P138 Wooden egg enameled black. Well scarred from much use. 3". $5.00

P139 Large wooden egg stained purple. Much used. From Switzerland. 3 1/4" $7.50

P140 Medium sized egg laminated with three pieces of wood. Decorated with Swiss emblem, a white cross on a red shield. From Switzerland. 2 1/2". $9.00

P141 Elongated goose size egg colorfully enameled with white, cream, green, red and blue swirls. Impressed "Made in Germany." 3". $12.50

Plate 136

Plate 137

Plate 138

Plate 139

Plate 140

Plate 141

P142   Small egg with flat butt. Enameled white. $5.00

Natural

P143   Medium sized egg, nicely grained, lightly varnished cedar. 3$^{1/8}$". $7.50

P144   Large wooden egg stained purple. Much used. From Switzerland. 3$^{1/4}$". $7.50

P145   Medium sized elongated egg, hickory. 3$^{1/4}$". $5.00

P146   Medium sized egg, oak. Heavily scarred from much usage. Came from the medieval village of Riquewihr, Alsace, France. 2$^{3/4}$". $10.00

P147   Small sized egg heavily scarred from much usage. Came from a swap meet in Madrid, Spain. 2$^{5/8}$" $10.00

P148   Medium sized egg, unfinished. This darner was purchased in Vernou, France from The Mill By the Woods, a "dealer in crockery, rustic furniture, household goods, knickknacks curios, rarities" and a horse breeder. Described as "An egg of wood intended for darning socks or the elbows of pullovers." 2$^{7/8}$". $12.50

P149   Side view. Small oblate sphere. Unfinished natural wood. Heavily used. 1$^{1/4}$".

P150   Top view of P149

Plate 142

Plate 143

Plate 144

Plate 145

Plate 146

Plate 147

Plate 148

Plate 149

Plate 150

Capsules

P151   (a) Mid sized capsule shape. Unfinished birch. 2⁷⁄₈". $4.50

       (b) Small sized "horse capsule" shape. Lightly varnished maple wood. Designed to drop into glove finger. 3/4" diameter, 1¹⁄₂" long. $3.50

       (c) Large sized capsule shape. Unfinished oak. 4". $6.50

Cones/Pestles

P152   Medium sized pestle shape. Lightly varnished beech. 3³⁄₈". $5.00

P153   Large sized cone shape. Lightly varnished Lignum Vitae wood which is very hard and so heavy it will not float in water. 4". $12.50

Balls

P154   (a) Round wooden ball coated with green plastic. Has nail hole from being attached to a "Coating Board" for dipping in plastic. This darner came from Murren, Switzerland where it was purchased in a dry goods store. It is called a "Strumpf Kugel" which is German for "Stocking Ball." 2¹⁄₄" $7.50
       (b) Round wooden ball coated with red plastic. See above. $7.50

P155   "Door knob" style with convex top and concave bottom. Groove around outside of knob suggests that, combined with a spring, it could be a fabric holder.

However, patent illustrations show the groove vacant with no spring. Varnished maple. To be used without a handle. Called a "darning form" and sometimes referred to as a "darning knob." Marked:

CUPPED BOTTOM
FACILITATES PICKING UP THREADS
BOYE
THIS SURFACE
DARNING FORM
THE BOYE NEEDLE CO. CHICAGO
MADE IN U.S.A. PAT. NO. D103715

This darner has a design patent issued to William A. Davis, Chicago, Illinois on July 31, 1936. 1¹⁄₄" $17.50

P156   Wooden wheel with groove around the rim. Marked:

NO-DARN
REG. U.S. PAT. OFFICE
CHICAGO

This device is not a darner in the usual sense. Rather it is a base for iron-on patches. Inserted into the sock, it served as an "ironing board." The patches were of cotton and came in various colors and sizes. A spiral wire spring was not used in conjunction with the groove to create a fabric holding darner. 1¹⁄₄". Advertised in a 1944 Sears Roebuck catalogue at 28 cents including 40 iron-on patches in assorted colors and sizes. $7.50

Plate 151

Plate 152

Plate 153

Plate 154

Plate 155

Plate 156

81

P157   Wooden wheel with grove around the rim. Marked:
NO-DARN
REG. US.
PATENT OFF.
SOCKS & HOSE
MENDING KNOB

As with P156, this device is not a "darner" but rather a "mender." This version has a hole in the rim of the wheel for attaching a dowel handle. It is sometimes called a "lollipop" darner. 1 1/8" $8.00

HOLLOW EGGS, COMPENDIUMS AND THIMBLE CASES

Souvenirs

P158   Egg shaped screw threaded compendium containing 2 spools, thimble and needle holder. Varnished dark, streaked olive wood presumptively from the Mount of Olives. Imprinted "JERUSALEM." 2 3/4". (Enlarged to show detail.) $35.00

P159   Egg shaped screw threaded compendium containing 2 spools, thimble and needle holder. Lightly varnished olive wood. This darner is marked "Sorrento" and is from Sorrento, Italy a port city southwest of Rome on the Bay of Naples. It was owned by a lady named Shermerthorn of Chappaquidick, Massachusetts who said it had been in her family since she was a little girl, and who gave it to Dr. Lucyle Hook of Barnard College in 1936, which would suggest that it was made around 1870. 2 3/4". (Enlarged to show detail.) $35.00

P160   Hollow, friction closed egg of bass wood. It is pyrographed: "For Ruth . . . Souvenir Revere Beach 1906." Revere Beach is about 6 miles north of Boston on the Atlantic Ocean. At the turn of the century it was a very popular recreation area with a large amusement park including a Ferris wheel and a roller coaster called "The Cyclone." Today it is still a popular beach but the amusement park has been replaced by condominiums. Pyrography is the art of burning designs on wood, leather, etc. 2 1/2". (Enlarged to show detail.) $35.00

Plate 157

Plate 158

Plate 159

Plate 160

P161   Large Friction closed egg of lightly varnished beech wood. Well used. Marked in old German script "ISCHL." Bad Ischl is a resort town in Austria about 35 miles east of Salsburg and about 185 miles southwest of Vienna in "Upper Austria." Bad Ischl contains "Kaiserville," the summer retreat of former Emperor Franz Joseph, and the villa and a museum commemorating composer Franz Lehar.

Darners are called by different names in German, just as they are in English. One is "Stopfen Kugel" or "mending ball." Or "Stopholz" which could translate to "mending wood." (Enlarged to show detail.) $35.00

Hollow Eggs - Varnished, Stained, Enameled

P162   Large hollow egg. Stained red and lightly varnished. Could be bee's wax holder.

Gertrude Whiting in "Olde Time Tools and Toys of Needlework" says: "I wonder if your workbag boasts . . . an egg of wax in an oval wooden darning ball that unscrews midway to give access to the wax therein?" $30.00

P163   Hollow friction-closed egg. Enameled yellow with two paintings of floral bouqets. Worn and chipped from much usage. English 2⁷/₈". $10.00

P164   Small globular friction-closed thimble case. Sycamore wood. 1½". $7.50

P165   Small egg shaped thimble case with metal closure. Enameled yellow with blue, red and gray. Marked "Made in Germany." (Enlarged to show detail.) $22.50

Mauchline and Tartanware

Mauchline is a Scottish ware developed in the 1820's in the town of Mauchline in Ayrshire. Originally pictures were drawn directly on the wood with India ink. By the 1830's the wood items were decorated with transferred engravings this is referred to as "transferware." Mauchline also includes Scotch plaids, called "Tartanware," "Fernware," "Seaweed," and "Floral" ware. Originally this type of wooden ware was not called "Mauchline" but rather such things as "white wood work" (from the light colored sycamore wood usually utilized), "Scotch goods," and "clan tartan wood work."

P166   Small Mauchline transferware friction-closed compendium containing 2 spools, needle holder and thimble. Sycamore wood. The transferred engraving is captioned "The Tower of London." 2⅛". (Enlarged to show detail.) $50.00

Plate 161

Plate 162

Plate 163

Plate 164

Plate 165

Plate 166

P167 Small Mauchline transferware friction-closed compendium containing 2 track spool, needle holder and thimble. Sycamore wood. The transferred engraving is captioned "Nave. Crystal Palace." The Crystal Palace was the main feature of the Great Exhibition held in London in 1851. The Exhibit was sponsored by Queen Victoria's husband, Prince Albert, to "wed high art with mechanical skill" and was built in Hyde Park in the center of London to house 100,000 objects sent by 5,000 exhibitors from all over the world. The "Palace" was designed by Jospeh Paxton and was the first prefabricated building, 95% built dismantled and re-erected as a center for popular entertainment, a forerunner of today's theme park, on a larger scale containing 50% more cubic space, at Sydenham in South London. It was destroyed in a spectacular fire in 1936. $2^{1/8}$". (Enlarged to show detail.) $55.00

P168 Small Mauchline transferware friction-closed compendium containing two-track spool, needle holder and thimble. Transferred engraving is of a rocky escarpment with profile of a man's head and face at the top. It is captioned "Enthroned in the clouds." (Enlarged to show detail.) 2". $50.00

P169 Small Mauchline Tartanware friction-closed compendium containing two-track spool, needle holder and thimble. Marked "Caledonia" which is the Roman name for Scotland. These small compendia have been called "Darning Crickets." 2". (Enlarged to show detail. $75.00

P170 Larger Mauchline transferware friction-closed compendium containing needle holder. Thimble and spools missing. Pictures a large house or inn. Captioned "Tip Top House, Mt. Washington, N.H." As is not unusual for well used enameled transferware darners the varnish and transfer are chipped. $2^{1/2}$". $20.00

P171 Larger Mauchline transferware friction-closed compendium containing needle holder. Thimble and spools missing. Pictures a large institution. Captioned "State Sanitarium, Raybrook, N.Y." Varnish and transfer are chipped from much use. $2^{1/2}$" $20.00

P172 Mid-size egg shaped compendium imprinted with a devil in red, green, yellow and blue colors. Contains three-track spool, needle holder and blue plastic thimble which protrudes through end of darner. Push on the thimble to open egg. Marked "Reg. Pat. No. 18434." This patent was issued to Conrad Woge of New York, NY on July 3, 1926 for what he called a "Kit of Sewing Outfits or the Like." He claimed "this invention relates to articles of manufacture and has for its object to provide a kit for sewing or knitting outfits which will be compact, durable and which can be conveniently carried in one's pocket or bag, without taking up much space." $2^{1/2}$" $35.00

P173 P172 opened.

Plate 167

Plate 168

Plate 169

Plate 170

Plate 171

Plate 172

Plate 173

P174 Clear plastic egg compendium, light amber color. Contains five plastic spools of thread, white plastic thimble, paper tape measure, four buttons, two snaps, safety pins and needles. Marked: "TRINA - Hong Kong" $25.00

P175 Small egg shaped screw-threaded compendium of root wood. Contains ivory needle holder with screw-on cap. Spool and thimble missing. $25.00

P176 Small bullet shaped compendium of brass and aluminum. Enameled cream and green. Contains 2-track spool, brass thimble and needle holder with metal cap. Marked "Made in Germany." $22.50

P177 Large egg shaped needle case. Push on bottom to open case. Turn dial to release size needle desired, from #5 to #9. Directions state "Place the stroke [arrow] parallel with the number required." Outside of egg shows a picture of a lady using a needle case and is marked "The Columbia Egg," "NEEDLE CASE," "Art. 1492," "GLORIA Trade Mark," and "Made in Germany." $2^{7/8}$". $75.00

P178 Bullet shaped compendium. Varnished maple wood. Contains 5 separate spools of thread, needle holder and thimble. This was an advertising premium for Michelin Tires. Carries two representations of the Michelin Man and is marked:

Tires
MICHELIN
Tubes
One Quality Only
Bluff City Garage and Filling Station
Phone 3-9294   M.M. Moody, Prop.
Parkway & Lauderdale   Memphis, Tenn.

Five digit phone number suggests 1930's. $3^{1/8}$". $40.00

P179 Egg shaped compendium on a pedestal. This is Mauchline transferware depicting "Dunham Cathedral From River." It contains a brass thimble, ivory needle case and ivory bodkin set in a velvet covered holder. English. $4^{1/4}$". $100.00

P180 P179 opened.

Plate 174

Plate 175

Plate 176

Plate 177

Plate 178

Plate 179

Plate 180

FABRIC HOLDER DARNERS -
CLIPS / SPRINGS / ELASTICS / BRUSHES

One objective of some darner makers was to devise a tool that would hold the fabric being darned so that it would not move during the darning process. This eliminated the necessity to hold the material tightly and thus tire the hand. It helped prevent stretching of the fabric which could result in a distorted darn. It enabled the darnee to lay the work aside to resume it later, without disturbing the position of the darn. Devices used include a metal "bicycle clip" or "pants guard," spiral spring, rubber or elastic band, short bristled plastic or wire "brush," and a high pile fabric facing.

P181   Wheel with convex top and bottom on a handle, the bulbous end of which was also used as a darner for smaller items and in some models the handle was a needle holder. The "holder" is similar to a bicycle clip or pants guard. Enameled black. Marked "Pat'd Dec. 18, 1900." $4^{3/8}$". $20.00

This darner, patent #664,104, was invented by William H. Snyder of Canton, Ohio, who assigned one half to Charles R. Miller, also of Canton. It was designated as a "Darning Last."

This darner is advertised in the 1903 Sears, Roebuck Catalogue as follows: "Queen Stocking and Glove Darner. Made of black ebonized wood, nickel plated spring to hold stocking or other fabric firmly in place. Does not require to be adjusted until work is completed. Price, each . . . 7 cents. Per dozen . . . 75 cents. If by mail, postage extra . . . 4 cents."

This darner was also advertised by John Little & Co., Ltd. of Singapore in 1910 as follows: "The 'QUEEN' DARNER. Makes hosiery mending a pleasure."

P182   Wheel with convex top and bottom on a handle, with bicycle clip fabric holder. This is the "varnished" model of the black enameled Snyder darner patented on December 10, 1900. $4^{3/8}$". $20.00

P183   One piece wheel with bulbous needle holder handle. Bicycle clip fabric holder. Varnished natural wood. $3^{1/2}$". $20.00

P184   Mushroom on grooved handle. Thin bicycle clip fabric holder with rounded ends. Marked RD No. 563612. $45.00

P185   Bulbous wheel with wide groove for spring or elastic fabric holder, on handle. Varnished natural wood. 5"   Paper label: $45.00

"Stoppspannare
Lilltorpslojden
Stockholm
Patent"
Lill = Little
Torp = Houe in the Country
Slojden = Handcraft articles

Translation:
"Darning Stretcher
Little Village Handcrafts
Stockholm
Patent"

Plate 181

Plate 182

Plate 183

Plate 184

Plate 185

P186   The TRICK darner. Mushroom on handle with spiral spring fabric holder. Varnished natural wood. Cap is detachable and reversible with one concave side and one convex side. The instruction card with the darner stated: "Darning and embroidery done quickly and easily without tired fingers. Use TRICK 25 cents. Patent Pending." Ca 1920. 4 7/8". $45.00

P187   Small mushroom with spiral spring fabric holder. Handle is glove darner. Varnished natural wood. 3 1/4" $17.50

P188   Ellipsoid "door knob" darner with spiral spring fabric holder, on handle. Enameled black. 4 3/4"

On April 15, 1890, Charles C. Gale of Glenville, Ohio was granted patent number 425,606, which he assigned to Eliza J. Gale of Cleveland, Ohio, for a "Darning Last" incorporating a "spring to retain the fabric," however this was probably not the first use of a spring fabric holder. $20.00

P189   Ellipsoid "door knob" darner with spiral spring fabric holder, on handle. Varnished natural wood. 4 7/8" $20.00

P190   "Door knob" style with spiral spring fabric holder. Varnished natural wood. Box is printed: "The Ebor Darner, Pat No. 231402. Made in England." This darner was patented at the British Patent office on April 2, 1925 by John Walter Kelley, a British subject of 5 Orchard Street, York, England. It is called a "Darning Device." A part of this implement was a "shedding pin," an enlongated metal object which, when turned, alternately raised and lowered the darning threads in the manner of a loom. Thus this type of darner was sometimes called a "loom darner." The knob has "slits or slots cut therein" but no purpose for these slots is given, although they might serve as visual guides for lining up the shedding pin. This darner is similar to another English loom darner called "The Daga." $30.00

P191   Mushroom with elastic fabric holder on bulbous handle. Cap is enameled black with hand painting of a girl in a peasant dress. Colors red, green, gold, brown, and black. Handle is painted red with decorations of black, green, yellow and white. Handle contains needle holder and thimble. Marked "Hungary P Hj." Original elastic has been replaced. 4 3/4"
                                                                                                                                                $45.00

On May 23, 1882, George A. Cochrane of New York, NY was granted patent #258,378 for a "conoidal" shaped darner using a "moderately-thick rubber ring" to hold the fabric. "The darning lasts now used are devoid of means for connecting the article firmly therewith."

Plate 186

Plate 187

Plate 188

Plate 189

Plate 190

Plate 191

P192   Ellipsoid shape with elastic fabric holder on a bulbous egg shaped handle. The ellipsoid end is enameled black (for light colored stockings) and the egg is varnished light wood (for dark colored stockings). The elastic fabric holder functioned regardless of which end of the darner was being used. $4^{1/8}$". $25.00

P193   Black enameled wooden egg shell, with the top cut off, on a handle. Sliding the shell down the handle reveals the plastic bristles of a brush. When in use the brush pushes against the stocking and keeps it from shifting. Also it does not allow the fabric to stretch. In addition, it protects the needle from dulling because it moves through the bristles instead of scraping across the top of a hard surface darner. As one inventor put it, "Heretofore it has been generally considered that a smooth hard surface was an essential quality in a darning last, in order that the point of the needle used in darning should not catch in the material on which the fabric to be darned was supported. I have found, however, that a surface composed of fibers vertically disposed and free at their outer ends, like the bristles of a brush, is much superior to a smooth surface as a support for the fabric being darned, for the reason that such fibers, while fully supporting the fabric to be darned and resisting its lateral displacement, offer no resistance to the passage of the needle, and as the fabric to be darned is to lifted from its support, as is the case when a smooth surface is employed, there is no stretching of the fabric darned, which is a point of importance in darning fine linen and similar goods."

On August 26, 1884, patent number 304,030 was issued to Charles E. Rames of Chicago, Illinois for a kindred device. Comparable darners, such as the English Marvel darner have metal "bristles" like a wire brush. $50.00

DARNERS OF CELLULOID, BAKELITE, IVORY, PLASTIC

Today most man-made materials in this category are referred to generically as "plastic." However "plastic" is a fairly recent name applied to many varieties of this material that have been developed through the years. Cellulose nitrate was invented by brothers J.W. Hyatt and I.S. Hyatt in 1868. The trade name "Celluloid" became accepted as the generic name for cellulose nitrate. It was phased out by the 1940's because it was quite flammable and because of newer developments. Cellulose acetate was similar to Celluloid, but without the flammability. Phenol formaldehyde, or Bakelite, was invented by L.H. Baekland in 1908, followed by other varieties of "plastic." Celluloid eggs on handles were advertised for 25 cents in 1904 and 23 cents in 1909.

P194   Celluoid (Ivorene) egg on handle decorated with ribbon bows and garlands of flowers. $6^{1/8}$". $30.00

P195   Cellulose acetate egg on handle. Egg is marbelized in beige and gold in a product called "Marbelette," an imitation marble, which was very popular. Handle is red and is bent, probably from being overheated, and then broken off. $4^{1/4}$" $15.00

P196   Celluloid egg on handle. Top of egg and handle is white. Bottom of egg is red. American made. $5^{3/4}$". $10.00

P197   Bakelite mushroom on handle. Marbleized gray and white. Cap unscrews for needle and thimble holder. Handle is glove darner. English." $3^{3/4}$". $35.00

Plate 192

Plate 193

Plate 194

Plate 195

Plate 196

Plate 197

P198 Bakelite mushroom on handle. Marbleized brown color. Cap unscrews for needle and thimble holder. Marked:"Made in England." 3¾" $35.00

P199 Red plastic mushroom on glove darner handle. Cap unscrews for needle holder. Marked with a depiction of a jay bird and: $22.50

> TRADE MARK
> A
> JAY BRAND
> PRODUCT
> MADE IN ENGLAND

P200 Plastic mushrooms on turned wooden handles. One mushroom cap is red, one is green. Handles are wood, enameled white and detachable. These are new darners purchased in Austria, where they are still being sold in dry goods stores and at notions counters. 4⅛". Each $10.00

P201 Small celluloid mushroom with red spots on cap and ivory colored screw-on glove darner and needle holder handle. 3⅛" $201.00

P202 Plastic. Beehive with glove darner handle. One side is white, marked "For dark material"; one side is green, marked "For light material." Handle is marked "Hungerford Darn-Aid Pats. Pending" and

> "For Glove
> - - - - - - - - - ->
> Fingers."

This darner was patented on May 31, 1949 by Daniel C. Hungerford of Madison, NJ and assigned to Hungerford Plastics Corporation of New Providence, NJ. He stated "One of the objects of my invention is the provision of such a device, different portions of the external surface of which are of strongly contrasting colors, light and dark respectively, in order to provide contrast between supporting surface of the device and the material or fabric being mended, regardless of the color of the latter." These darners were manufactured in several different contrasting colors combinations. 5¾". $17.50

Other darners with contrasting colors were a wooden reversible darner patented on March 11, 1913 by Richard Nelson of Chicago, Illinois, and a metal "clam shell" type patented on May 4, 1926 by Daniel W. Causey of Norfolk, Virginia.

P203 Plastic. Beehive with glove darner handle. One side is white and one side is red. This is also a "Hungerford" darner in one of the many color combinations which were made. 5¾" $17.50

Plate 198

Plate 199

Plate 200

Plate 201

Plate 202

Plate 203

P204   Plastic semi foot-form on glove darner handle. Marked "Made in U.S.A." and "Pat. Pend." This darner was mass produced in molds and various colors. 6". Shown here in white, blue and pink. (each) $12.50

P205   Plastic semi foot-form on glove darner handle. One half is white (for dark stockings) and one half is a darner color (for light colored stockings.) Mass produced in molds and various colors. 6". Shown here in white with maroon, purple and red. (each) $12.50

P206   (a) Small fossilized walrus ivory egg on handle, highly polished. Handle unscrews. From Alaska. $80.00

(b) Ivory miniature elongated egg on handle. This darner was hand carved for a doll house. 5/8". $27.50

P207   Small polished ivory mushroom type darner with concave cap and grooved proper knop on end of handle. Out of an English Regency sewing casket. From Gillingham, Dorset, England. CA 1830. $60.00

P208   Celluloid egg with pale blue butt end and ivory colored (Ivorene) narrow end. 2½" $15.00

P209   Plastic half footform. Black with painted lady in long, white, flowing dress. Opens to contain sewing articles. Marked inside:
"Darning Egg
British Made
Patent NO 600975"

This darner was patented on April 23, 1948 by Julius Mendle and Moritz Mendle of Porth, Rhondda, Glamorganshire, Wales who were both of German nationality. It is made of "thermo plastic material" and they called the shape a "flattened bee-hive" with a flattened base so that it "may be stood upright so that it will not roll away." In the hollow interior "darning or sewing requisites can be housed." 3". $30.00

Plate 204

Plate 205

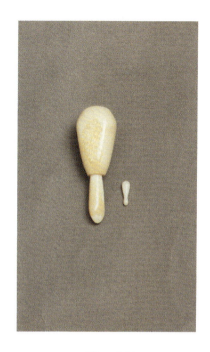

Plate 206

Plate 207

Plate 208

Plate 209

P210 Yellow plastic round box with dome shaped cap. Cap unscrews for storage space for a handle which inserts into the cap to form a mushroom type darner. Handle is also a needle case with screw-open cap. Marked: "Always Darn With 'GLISTA' Yarn," and "Made in England." This was most likely a promotional item for the sale of "Glista" yarn and may have contained spools of it. $2^{3/4}$" $30.00

P211 P210 opened.

ODDITIES

P212 Natural, unfinished wood. This is a Shaker device called "Ball and Block" or "Ball and Socket." It consists of a free moving ball inset into a round block of wood. The ball and the block are of two different woods and no seams are evident to enable insertion of the ball into the block. When used in darning, the ball turned with the needle thrusts so that the needle did not scrape across the top, thus it was more "efficient," and efficiency in all their endeavors was an objective of the Shakers. There is a somewhat larger version of this darner in the Shaker Museum in Old Chatham, NY believed to be from the Shaker Village at Mt. Lebanon, NY which was founded in 1787. $1^{1/2}$". $100.00

P213 Tin tube with a rounded cap at each end. Cap on one end comes off to provide storage space inside the darner. This darner was a promotional item for Paragum Mending Paste which it contained. It is grain-painted to resemble light colored wood and is marked "Paragum [Trade Mark] DARNER and Receptacle for Paragum [Trade Mark] MENDING PASTE. Swanson Supply Co. Seattle, U.S.A." Gertrude Whiting in *Old Time Tools & Toys of Needlework* mentions "gums" for stopping runs in stockings. $4^{1/4}$" $35.00

P214 Plastic mushroom with pink cap and brown stem. This is a battery-powered darner. The cap is removable to permit access to the batteries and bulb. Marked "Darn-A-Lite" and "Made in England" where it is called a "darning torch." $4^{1/2}$". $50.00

P215 Plastic mushroom with white cap and red handle with a cord leading out of the end of it to an English style electrical plug. The box is marked "Pifco Electric Darner, Cat. No. 987, 200-250 Volts, AC only. Made in England." "Makes Light work of Darning." $4^{3/8}$".
                                                                                        $75.00

Plate 210

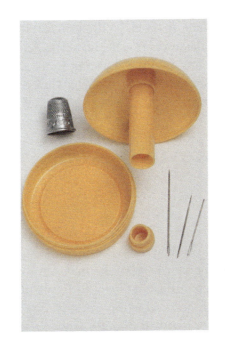

Plate 211

Plate 212

Plate 213

Plate 214

Plate 215

P216   Singer Stocking Darner. This is a metal device with a coiled spiral spring fabric holder which holds the hole in the fabric in the center of the oblong implement, and with six moveable hooks into which the rest of the stocking is rolled and secured, so as to permit darning on a lock-stitch sewing machine. It is claimed to ". . . enable you to darn socks and stockings easier and better than by hand. Will not harm the stocking, and machine-made darns will not hurt the feet. Requires no special skill. A little practice is all that is required to darn successfully." It was used with a "darning foot" attachment. This type of Singer device was in use in 1923. Singer also offered what they called a "flat darner" for "repairing holes in table clothes, blankets and other woven material" by use of the sewing machine.
$35.00

WOODEN EGGS ON HANDLES OTHER THAN WOOD

Silver Handles

The concept of attaching silver handles to darners seems to have been a peculiarity of the United States and they were seldom found elsewhere. Most silver handles on darners are "Sterling" although some are "silver plated." The word "sterling" may have derived indirectly from the name "Eaterling," who were German silversmiths who went to England in the Middle Ages. Or perhaps from the starling (little star) used in the production of early English silver. But the word used in identifying silver of a certain quality evolved directly from the English coin which was called a "sterling."

Many of the silver handles are not identifiable because they were not standard patterns of silversmiths, but rather were special order, "private label" designs, and do not bear the makers' marks. Some attribution may be inferred, at least as to approximate date, by comparing the patterns to known designs, and a few may be identified by their marks. These would include Durgin Silver company, Concord, New Hampshire; Foster & Bailey, Providence, Rhode Island; International Silver Company, East Boston, Massachusetts; La Pierre Manufacturing Company, New York, New York; Shreve & Company, San Francisco, California; Redall & Company, and Unger Brothers of Newark, New Jersey; Mandalien & Hawkings, Palmer & Peckham, and Webster Company, of North Attleboro, Massachusetts.

Ebony

On darners with handles other than wood, and particularly silver handled darners, the eggs often are ebony. Ebony is a very hard, black wood that was first imported from the East Indies in the late 16th century. There was also "green ebony" which was probably ash and Bois Noirci or "ebonized wood" which was wood stained black from which furniture was made.

In addition to darners, ebony was used for boxes, piano keys, cabinets, tables and chairs although it is brittle and very costly. Ebony was also used in very thin strips, perhaps 1/32nd of an inch as dividers between pieces of light wood.

Large Black Eggs on Silver Handles

P217   Ebony egg on very large silver repousse handle marked sterling. 6¾". $125.00

P218   Large ebony egg on silver repousse handle of roses. 6¾". CA 1895-1905. $100.00

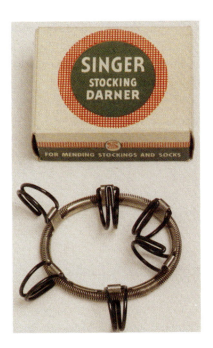

Plate 216

Plate 217 　　　　　　　　　　Plate 218

103

P219   Large ebony pear on silver engraved handle with small collar. Marked "Sterling." Engraved "F." 6¼". The hallmark is a "D" atop the blade of a dagger.

A catalogue of Shreve & Company of San Francisco in the late 1800's featured a darner with this identical handle. However, the egg is much rounder that the "pear" shape of this darner. It was carried in the section of silver needlework tools which included tape measures, embroidery hoops, needle cases, thimble cases, glove darners, stilletos, bodkins and housewives. It sold for $1.75. $100.00

P220   Large ebony egg on silver repousse handle. Marked "Sterling." 5⅝". $100.00

P221   Large ebony egg on large silver repousse handle. Marked "Sterling." 6". Ca 1880.
$95.00

P222   Large enameled wooden egg on silver repousse handle. Marked "Stelring." 6" Ca 1880.
$90.00

P223   Large ebony egg on ornate silver repousse handle and collar. Marked "Sterling B 34" and engraved "Flo." 6¼" $125.00

P224   Large ebony egg on silver repousse handle. Marked "Sterling." 6¼". CA 1890.
$100.00

P225   Large ebony egg on silver repousse handle. Marked "Sterling." Handle is slightly bent due to being caught in sewing machine or sewing box drawer. 6". CA 1885. $80.00

P226   Large ebony egg on beaded silver handle. Marked "Sterling." Engraved "S." Slightly bent due to being caught in drawer. 5⅞". $90.00

P227   Extra large ebony egg on silver respousse handle. Marked "Sterling." End of handle flattened from being dropped." 6". $75.00

Plate 219

Plate 220

Plate 221

Plate 222

Plate 223

Plate 224

Plate 225

Plate 226

Plate 227

P228   Large enameled wooden egg on medium silver repousse handle. Marked "Sterling." Tip of handle slightly dented from being dropped. 5½". Ca 1885. $85.00

P229   Large ebony egg on medium silver repousse handle with small collar. Marked "Sterling." 5½". Hallmark is the head of a bird on a long neck. CA 1895. $100.00

P230   Large ebony egg on silver engraved handle. Marked "Sterling" and "M &H." 5". This darner was made by Mandalian & Hawkins of North Attleboro, Massachusetts. CA 1910-1920. $100.00

P231   Large Ebony egg on small repousse handle. marked "Sterling." 5¼". CA 1900. $85.00

P232   Medium size ebony egg on small sterling silver repousse handle. marked "Sterlng." Ca 1890. $85.00

P233   Large ebony egg on small silver repousse handle. Mark indecipherable. 5". CA 1900. $85.00

Small Black Eggs on Silver Handles

P234   Small ebony egg on large silver repousse handle. Marked "F&B Sterling Pat'd." Engraved "F." 5⅝". Made by Theodore W. Foster & Bros. Co. This company was originally called Foster & Bailey and was founded in Providence, Rhode Island in 1873 by Theodore W. Foster and Samuel H. Bailey. In 1878 it became White, Foster & Co. From 1898 to 1951 it operated as Theodore W. Foster & Bros. Co.

The company made gold-filled, electroplated and sterling silver vanity cases, cigarette cases, clock cases ecclesiastical goods, cigar and cigarette holders, knives, medals, pens and pencils, photo frames, dresserware and candlesticks for which U.S. Patent #28,069, April 17, 1896 was registered. $100.00

Plate 228

Plate 229

Plate 230

Plate 231

Plate 232

Plate 233

Plate 234

P235   Small ebony egg on small silver repousse handle. Marked "Sterling." 4³/⁴" Ca 1890.
$80.00

P236   Small ebony egg on small silver repousse handle with small collar. Marked "Sterling." One side of egg is flattened to prevent darner from rolling. 5" Ca 1890. $90.00

P237   Small ebony egg on small silver repousse handle. Marked "Sterling." 5". Ca 1900
$85.00

P238   Small ebony egg on small silver repousse handle with large collar. Marked with a crown and "Sterling 925 Fine."

This darner was made by Reddall & Company of Newark, New Jersey. The "925 Fine" indicates that it is made of 925 parts pure silver and 75 parts alloy, out of 1000 parts. 4³/⁴". Ca 1896-1909. $100.00

P239   Small ebony egg on small silver repousse handle. Marked "Sterling." 4¹/⁴". Ca 1900. End flattened. $60.00

P240   Small enameled wooden egg on small silver repousse handle. Marked "Sterling." 4¹/⁴". Ca 1880. $65.00

P241   Small enameled wooden egg on small silver repousse handle the end of which is slightly flattened by being dropped. Marked "Sterling." 3³/⁴". Ca 1900. $60.00

Colored Eggs on Silver Handles

Although the eggs on some darners were enameled in colors other than black strictly for decorative appeal, there was a much more utilitarian reason for most of them. It was to provide contrast between the color of the fabric being darned and the darner head, thus enabling the darnee to see the work more clearly. If one were darning a dark stocking or fabric, a light darner would be used. If one were darning a light stocking or fabric, a dark darner would be used.

Plate 235

Plate 236

Plate 237

Plate 238

Plate 239

Plate 240

Plate 241

P242 Large white enameled egg on beaded silver handle with a collar. Marked "Sterling," and "P. & P.". This darner was manufactured by Palmer & Peckham of North Attleboro, Massachusetts. 6". Ca 1896-1904. $100.00

P243 Large white enameled egg on beaded silver handle. Marked "Sterling." Engraved "MW." The hallmark is a stylized "S" superimposed on a "D." Also marked STERLING 810S. This darner was manufactured by Durgin Silver company of Concord, New Hampshire. 5½". $100.00

P244 Large white enameled egg on medium repousse silver handle marked "Sterling." Hallmark indicates this darner was manufactured by International Silver Company. 5". Ca 1895. $100.00

P245 Small white enameled egg on small plain silver handle. Mark indecipherable. Engraved "A.H." 4 1/2"." Handle dented. $60.00

P246 Large maroon enameled egg on beaded silver handle. Maroon coloring is rare. 5½". $90.00

P247 Large green marbleized enameled egg on beaded silver handle. Marked "Sterling." 5¾". Ca 1885. This coloring, as opposed to black or white, was not applied primarily to provide contrast, but rather for decorative purposes and to enhance the eye appeal of this darner. $95.00

Composites

The eggs on some darners are composed of several pieces of wood, usually four, which were glued together with very thin layers of ebony separating them and then turned on a lathe to the desired shape. The wood typically was light colored and sometimes nicely grained. At the top of the egg was a mother-of-pearl (nacre) disc set in a circle of ebony. These embellishments served no practical purpose but did add to the visual appeal of the darners.

Plate 242

Plate 243

Plate 244

Plate 245

Plate 246

Plate 247

P248   Very large, elongated egg on silver handle. Composed of four sections of monkey wood separated by thin ebony layers. Mother-of-pearl disc inset in top of egg. Marked "Sterling Handle." $7^{1/4}$". Ca 1915-1920. $125.00

P249   Large egg with silver handle. Composed of four sections of olive wood separated by thin ebony layers. Mother-of-pearl disc inset in top of egg. $6^{1/4}$". Engraved "Violet." Marked "Sterling" and "Shreve & Co."

This darner was made by Shreve and Company of San Francisco which has been in business there since 1852. The handle is done in the "strap work" style with a hammered finish and is a Shreve pattern called "14th Century Standard." $150.00

Jeweled

P250   Large ebony egg on silver respousse handle decorated with 1/2 inche amethyst. Marked "Sterling." $6^{1/4}$". $150.00

In 1903, Sears, Roebuck & Company featured an "Amethyst set" darner at 68 cents, "if by mail, postage extra 5 cents."

Cartouches

The cartouche is an ornamented plaque with space for engraving and designed to be mounted on another object. In the case of darners, cartouches are silver and mounted on the handles. Also sometimes called a "shield."

P251   Large ebony egg on ebony handle with small silver cartouche marked "Sterling." Also marked "Warranted Real Ebony <k>." 6". $65.00

P252   Large ebony egg on ebony handle with annulated knop and large silver cartouche marked "Sterling." $6^{1/4}$". $70.00

Stag Horn

In the past, stag horn was popular as handles on a great many things including magnifying glasses, cutlery carving sets, dresser sets, letter openers, cork screws, hunting and pocket knives, and cheese scoops. Enterprising whittlers made whistles from stag horn.

The use of stag horn eventually declined due to a decreasing supply-fewer people hunted to put food on their tables- and because of the invention in 1868 of pyroxylin, the best known of which is Celluloid, and which manufacturers soon discovered could be shaped into any desired shape, including stag horns.

P253   Large ebony egg on stag horn handle. $6^{3/4}$". $100.00

Plate 248

Plate 249

Plate 250

Plate 251

Plate 252

Plate 253

P254 Large brown enameled egg on imitation stag horn handle, with a metal collar. There originally was a metal plate on the end of the handle for engraving. 6¹/₄₄". $90.00

Champleve

Champleve is somewhat similar to Cloisonne in appearance, but is different in that the design is depressed or incised into the metal rather than being built up with wire dividers as in the cloisonne procedure.

P255 Large ebony egg on green, white and red Champleve handle. 5½". $150.00

Mother of Pearl

Mother-of-pearl comes from the hard, smooth glossy lining of certain mollusk shells such as the pearl oyster, mussel and abalone. It changes colors as the light changes and is used to make various articles such as jewelry, ornaments and buttons.

Mother-of-pearl glass was also developed and with the creation of such man-made materials as cellulose acetate a form of "plastic" Mother-of-Pearl was developed. Companies making pearl handled wares included Meriden Britannia Company of Meriden, Connecticut about 1861.

P256 Large ebony egg on white Mother-of-Pearl handle, carved with stylized floral design. 5". $125.00

Art Nouveau

Art Nouveau is the French phrase for "New Art," a type of design that achieved popularity from approximately the 1880's to the early 1900's. It was characterized by long, sinuous, flowing lines and featured flowers, vines, snakes, insects and sensuous female forms with long flowing hair.

P257 Large ebony egg on silver repousse handle featuring an Art Nouveau lady with long hair. This darner is attributed to Unger Brothers Silversmiths, founded by the five Unger brothers in 1872. They made mostly pocket knives and hardware specialties and began making jewelry in 1878. In 1880, Emma Dickinson, the new wife of Eugene Unger began designing Art Nouveau articles for which they became famous.

The last Unger brother died in 1909 and the company stopped making Art Nouveau patterns in 1910. By 1914 they had stopped producing any silver and turned to making airplane parts. 5¾" $125.00

P258 Large white enameled egg on silver repousse handle and collar. The handle is Art Nouveau depicting a young lady with long, flowing hair. This darner was manufactured by Simons Brothers Company of Philadelphia, established in 1839. It was part of their "New Art" line and is marked "Sterling" and "1545" which is their style number. $150.00

Plate 254

Plate 255

Plate 256

Plate 257

Plate 258

GLOVE DARNERS

Silver

P259   (a) All silver darner with incised twist handle and small and larger eggs on opposite ends. Has loop for attaching to chatelaine. Marked "Sterling." Engraved. B.W.S." $4^{1/8}$"
$100.00

(b) All silver darner with different sized eggs on opposite ends of handle for different sized fingers. Note loop on handle for attaching to a chatelaine. $4^{1/2}$"

Marked "Sterling 1066" with hallmark of La Pierre Manufacturing Company which was started by Frank H. La Pierre in New York in 1888 and incorporated in New Jersey in 1895. Became part of International Silver Co., in 1929. Noted for novelites, small wares and dresserware. The La Pierre mark was made up of the sytlized letters F with superimposed L.
$100.00

P260   (a) All silver darner with standard egg on one end and pointed egg on other. Marked "Sterling." Handle bent from having drawer closed on it. $4^{5/8}$". This darner was featured in the 1915-16 catalogue of the Webster Company for 88 cents.
$75.00

(b) Silver flowered incised twist handle with large and small ebony eggs for different size fingers. Marked "Sterling." Made by Webster Company of North Attleboro, Massachusetts, which was founded by George K. Webster in 1869, and became a subsidiary of Reed & Barton in 1950. Principle products have been mostly baby goods, dresserware, picture frames, and sterling silver darners. $4^{1/2}$". Webster hallmark is a "W" with an arrow through it superimposed with "C o".
$110.00

Wood

P261   (a) Standard wood glove darner with large and small eggs. Enameled light blue. $4^{1/2}$".
$17.50

(b) Standard wood glove darner with large and small egg. Enameled white. $4^{3/8}$".
$17.50

P262   (a) Wood glove darner with two elongated eggs joined with a small proper knop. Enameled in marbelized caramel, brown and orange. 3".
$15.00

(b) Wooden rod shape with rounded ends. Hollow to serve as needle case. One end is 3/8" and cap is 1/2" in diameter. $4^{1/4}$"
$25.00

P263   (a) Oak wood baseball bat shape. One end is 3/4" and the other end is 1/2" in diameter. 6" long.
$25.00

(b) Unusually large wood glove darner enameled black. Enlongated smaller egg on one end of handle and large egg on other, quite large for a glove darner but too small for a stocking darner. $5^{5/8}$"
$25.00

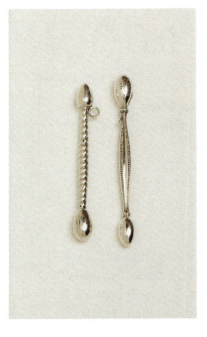

Plate 259

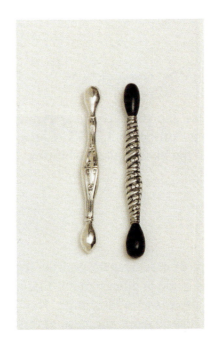

Plate 260

Plate 261

Plate 262

Plate 263

P264 This is a stocking darner and glove darner set. Marbleized caramel and brown. Glove darner has two eggs on a handle. 4½" long. Stocking darner is a ring over which fabric is stretched as with a darning hoop or drinking glass. 2" in diameter. Ribbon suggests the set was part of a homemade chatelaine. $25.00

GLASS

As indicated earlier, although glass darners were made at many glass companies, only a relatively small portion of them were part of the company's regular production output. Most glass darners are one-of-a-kind products of the glassblowers whimsey.

Nailsea

One of the first makers of this type of glass was the Nailsea factory near Bristol, England, in the 1780's although similar glass was made in other parts of England, Scotland, France, Germany and the Netherlands as well. It was also made in Pittsburgh, New jersey, New York and New England. "Nailsea" has become the generic name for glass of this type which is so many times called "looped glass" or "drape glass."

P265 Large ball on handle. Brown with white loopings. Cases. Sheared pontil mark. 7½". $450.00

P266 Large ball on handle. White with green loopings. Cased. Sheared pontil mark. 8¾". $500.00

P267 Large ball on handle. White with maroon loopings. Cased. Sheared pontil mark. 7⅛". $550.00

Cranberry Glass

Cranberry glass was being made in the early 1600's and became popular in the United States in the last half of the 1800's. The finest cranberry glass was made by adding gold to the molten glass which produced the color of cranberry juice. A lesser quality glass was produced by adding copper, instead of gold, to the mix. It is sometimes called "Ruby Glass."

P268 Ball on handle. Thick glass. Sheared pontil mark. 7½". $175.00

P269 Small ball on handle. Thick glass. Polished pontil mark. 5⅓". Pilgrim Glass Company. $150.00

Plate 264

Plate 265

Plate 266

Plate 267

Plate 268

Plate 269

P270 Pear shape on handle. Thick glass. Polished pontil mark. 5½". Pilgrim Glass Company.
$150.00

Milk Glass

Milk glass is a white, opaque glass named for its milky color. First made in England in the 1700's, it became very popular in the United States in the 1870's as tableware and novelties such as covered dishes with animal shaped lids. Other colors are now being referred to as "milk glass" such as "green milk glass," "blue milk glass," and "black milk glass." It is also sometimes called "Alabaster" glass, not to be confused with genuine alabaster which is a mineral much to soft to be used in a darner.

P271 Small round ball on handle. Free blown. Sheared pontil mark. 4 1/8". $100.00

P272 Ball on handle. Free blown. Unusual in that it is cased with a layer of clear glass over the white base. Sheared pontil mark. 5 3/4". $125.00

P273 Large ball on handle. Free blown. Thick, single layer glass. Ground pontil mark. 6 5/8".
$150.00

Porcelain

P274 One piece porcelain egg on handle. Egg is decorated with 20 hand painted yellow flowers with green leaves. Handle is ivory colored with gold band. Probably American Belleek. The Ceramic Art Company (predecessor of Lenox) catalogue of 1897 listed a stocking darner and a glove darner in plain white, inasmuch as painting china was a popular hobby in the late 1800's and early 1900's. 5 5/8". $50.00

P275 (a) Porcelain egg on black wood handle. Egg is decorated with sailing ship under full sail in blue, yellow and gold, with gold band at top of egg. Reverse side has four seagulls in blue, white and orange. 5 5/8". $50.00

(b) Porcelain egg on black wood handle. Egg is decorated with a bouquet of pink roses and green leaves. Gold ban around top of egg. Reverse side has a single pink rose on a green stem. 5 5/8". $50.00

Plate 270

Plate 271

Plate 272

Plate 273

Plate 274

Plate 275

Peachblow

The name "Peachblow" has been applied to different varieties of a certain type of art glass known as "shaded glass" which was developed to simulate the coloring of a fine Chinese glazed porcelain. Several American glass works, including Hobbs, Brockunier & Company, New England Glass Works, Mount Washington Glass Company (which became Pairpoint company and later Gunderson Glass Company), New Martinsville Glass Company, and Boston and Sandwich Glass Company made versions of this glass and marked it under different names.

P276   Pink ball shading to white handle. Single layer, free blown, sheared pontil mark. Glossy finish. New England Glass Works, Cambridge, Massachusetts. This darner was in a family named Brokaw since 1893. $6^{1/8}$" $250.00

P277   Pink ball shading to white handle. Single layer, free blown, sheared pontil mark. Glossy finish. New England Glass Works, Cambridge, Massachusetts. $5^{3/4}$". $250.00

Czechoslovakian Glass

Czechoslovakian has been long noted for its fine glass. Because of the excellent natural resources of glass industry has flourished in the area from the mid 1300's. The country was declared an independent republic in 1918 at the end of World War I as a result of the breakup of the Austro-Hungarian Monarchy. In 1993 it was redivided into the Czech and Slovakian republics.

P278   Pale blue egg on handle. Free blown. Ground and polished pontil mark. Etched "Czechoslovakia." These darners were produced in large quantities and several different colors. $5^{3/4}$" $75.00

P279   Amber colored egg on handle. Free blown. Ground and polished pontil mark. Etched "Czechoslovakia." Amber glass was especially popular in America just after the War Between the States around 1866. Amber glass was manufactured by many American companies including Stoddard Glass House of New Hampshire. $5^{3/4}$" $75.00

P280   Pale green egg on handle. Free blown. Ground and polished pontil mark. Etched "Czechoslovakia." $5^{3/4}$". $75.00

Cased

Cased glass is glass with layers of different colored glass and clear glass. There may be two, three or more layers, often with a white base and clear outer layer with colored layer(s) between. The flowing are just two examples of the many that appear in other glass categories in this chapter.

P281   Egg on handle. Pink base cased with clear glass. Free blown. Closed and polished pontil mark. $5^{3/4}$". $75.00

Plate 276 Plate 277 Plate 278

Plate 279 Plate 280 Plate 281

P282   Egg on handle. Pale blue base cased with clear glass. Free blown. Polished, open pontil mark. 5¾". $75.00

Powdered Glass

In producing this glass, the interior is coated with the desired color of powder and it is heated in the kiln to fix the color. It is colored in gold, copper, bronze, silver and white. Much of it was made in northwest Pennsylvania and southwest New York. This glass has been referred to as a variation of "Mercury Glass," which came in colors of silver, gold, aqua-blue and light pink. However Mercury Glass, or "Silvered Glass" is sealed between two layers of glass to avoid deterioration of the "silver."

P283   Oblate ball on glove darner handle. Single layer with white powdered interior. Free blown. Closed and polished pontil mark. 8⅛". $135.00

P284   Egg on glove darner handle. White powdered interior. Cased, white orange and blue bases. Free blown. Closed and polished pontil mark. 8⅛". $125.00

P285   Small oblate ball on glove darner handle. White loose powder. Cased, with spatters and strips of maroon, green, blue and pink. Free blown. Closed and polished pontil mark. 6¼" $90.00

P286   Very large inverted baluster shape on very long glove darner handle. This darner is strictly a glass blower's whimsey. Cased, with gold powdered interior and pea green blazes and stripes. Free blown. Closed and polished pontil mark. 13½". $225.00

P287   Large oblate ball on large glove darner handle. Cased, with gold powdered interior and bases of maroon and blue. Free blown. Closed and polished pontil mark. 9⅜". $200.00

P288   Large oblate ball on glove darner handle. Single layer with gold powdered interior. Free blown. Closed and polished pontil mark. 8". $175.00

Plate 282

Plate 283

Plate 284

Plate 285

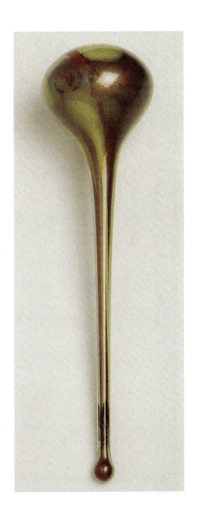

Plate 286

Plate 287

Plate 288

P289   Small ball on short handle. Handle is blown with a "twist." Very pale thick green glass with copper lining. Free blown. Sheared open pontil mark. 4½". $40.00

P290   Ball on handle. Thin clear glass with copper lining. Free blown. Sheared open pontil mark. Sometimes inaccurately called "Mercury Glass" or "Luster Glass." 5⅛" $50.00

Clear Glass

Clear glass is a transparent glass to which no color has been added, however it may sometimes have a tinge of green, yellow or brown as a result of the ingredients used in its manufacture. Some glass makers consider a perfect item in clear glass to be the ultimate expression of glass artistry.

P291   Small ball on handle. One layer. Free blown. Snapped pontil mark. 5¼". $50.00

P292   Small ball on handle with ball knop. One layer. Free blown. Snapped pontil mark.. Repaired. 5". $35.00

P293   Ball on long handle. One layer. Free blown. Snapped pontil mark. 7". $65.00

P294   Ball on long bulbous handle. One layer. Free blown. Snapped pontil mark. 7¾".
                                                                                $75.00

P295   Ball on handle. Very thick, one layer. Free blown. Glass has slight greenish tint and contains several "seeds" possibly suggesting early date of production. Handle is lightly ribbed and twisted. Snap pontil mark. $75.00

P296   Pear shape tapering into very long glove darner type handle. Free blown. Closed and polished pontil mark. 12¾" $150.00

Plate 289   Plate 290

Plate 291

Plate 292

Plate 293

Plate 294

Plate 295

Plate 296

Clear Glass with Color Blazes

P297 Pear shape tapering into very thick glove darner type handle. Swirls of maroon, blue and white. Free blown. Closed and polished pontil mark. $7^{1/8}$". $145.00

P298 Large oblate ball on long, thick glove darner type handle. Blazes of maroon, orange and light blue on ball. Handle is clear glass. Free blown. Closed and polished pontil mark. $7^{1/2}$". $155.00

P299 Pear shape tapering into glove darner type handle. Very faint white blazes. Free blown. Closed and polished pontil mark. $7^{1/2}$". $135.00

Glass Mushrooms

P300 Clear glass. Free blown. Closed and polished pontil mark. $3^{7/8}$". $45.00

P301 Cased glass with swirls of blue, yellow and white from the center of the cap down the handle. Cased with blue tinge glass. Free blown. Closed and ground pontil mark. $3^{1/4}$". $50.00

Glass Foot Forms

P302 Small blue glass foot form. Mold blown. Has a nippled, closed pontil mark. Rippled interior. $57.00

Large numbers of these small darners were made in many colors. All have smooth exteriors and slightly rippled interiors. The 1942-43 catalogue from Daniel Low's of Salem, Massachusetts advertised them as follows:

"KRISTL"
New streamline darner of clear, smooth
glass in lovely green, blue, for fine
silk hosiery, curved to fit hand. $5^{1/4}$ in
N 224. 3 for 1.00. Three useful pretty gifts.

Plate 297

Plate 298

Plate 299

Plate 300

Plate 301

Plate 302

129

P303   Small blue glass foot form. Mold blown. Has a dimpled, closed pontil mark. Rippled interior. Length 5"; width 2 1/8"; thickness 1 3/4". $57.00

While these darners were blown in the same sized molds, the closed pontil marks range from dimples to nipples which were individually hand finished, which accounts for the differences in length.

P304   Small green glass foot form. Mold blown. Has closed, nippled pontil mark. 5 5/16". (See P302/303). $57.00

P305   Small amethyst glass foot form. (See P302/303). $57.00

P306   Small light blue glass foot form. (See P302/303). $57.00

P307   Large green cased glass foot form.. The inner layer is green, rippled glass and the outer layer is clear, smooth glass. Closed and polished pontil mark. 5 1/2" long; 2 5/8" wide; and 1 5/8" thick. $110.00

Cobalt Glass

Cobalt glass was made as early as the Renaissance Age, 1300-1500, by Venetian glass makers and later in other areas including England, especially Bristol, and in the United States. Among American makers were Pairpoint Manufacturing Company of New Bedford, Massachusetts, Corning Glass Works and several Pittsburgh glass makers. Tiffany's cobalt blue was especially notable. The bright, dark blue color was obtained by adding oxide of cobalt to the mix.

P308   Ball on handle. One layer. Free blown. Ground pontil mark. Needle marks indicate usage. 7" $165.00

Plate 303

Plate 304

Plate 305

Plate 306

Plate 307

Plate 308

P309   Large "frosted" cobalt ball on handle, overlaid with clear glass. Free blown. Snapped pontil mark. The ball is frosted in white glass with "Home Sweet Home" and a depiction of a mill building, a tree, a pump and a pond with reeds and a swan. The lettering and illustration was cut into a steel die which was filled with powdered glass, or "frit," which was picked up with a glove of molten glass. The frit for any given article may be all of the same color, or of several different colors. This particular motif was used on other objects such as paperweights. $6^{3/4}$"

Venetian Glass

Venetian glass was produced on the island of Murano, near Venice as early as the thirteenth century. It is a thin, delicate ware incorporating many colors, flecks of gold or silver, and often applied decorations.

P310   Ball on handle. Multicolored with red, blue, pink, olive and white, and flecked with gold. Cased on a light blue base; Very light weight. Top of ball and handle are swirled. Handle is encircled with a pink crenulation akin to glass rickrack, sometimes called "rigaree," "rigaree trail" or "cake icing." This darner came from an estate in the Mother Lode in California and had been in the family since the 1800's. $4^{7/8}$". $700.00

Bottle Glass

The bottle factories produced an inexpensive glass in different colors including brown, blue, green, white and clear. The glass blowers, on their own time, often made novelty items including darners.

P311   Brown bottle glass pear shape darner. Free blown. One layer. Snapped pontil mark. 7". $100.00

P312   Brown bottle glass ball on handle. Heavy, thick glass. Free blown. One layer. Snapped pontil mark. $6^{1/8}$" $100.00

P313   Brown bottle glass ball on handle. Heavy, very thick glass. Free blown. One layer. Snapped pontil mark. $6^{1/8}$" $100.00

Amber Glass

Amber glass is the designation for any glassware with the appropriate yellow-brown color. It was produced by adding carbon or charred oats to the molten glass. It was particularly popular after the Civil War.

P314   Amber glass "door knob" on bulbous handle. Free blown. One layer. Closed and polished pontil mark. Etched "Czechoslovakia." $4^{1/2}$". $100.00

Plate 309

Plate 310

Plate 311

Plate 312

Plate 313

Plate 314

P315   Amber glass "door knob" shape darner. Free blown. One layer. Ground pontil mark. $5^{3/8}$".
$100.00

P316   Amber glass ball on handle. Free blown. One layer. Snapped pontil mark. $6^{1/8}$".
$100.00

Green Glass

Green glass was produced by adding copper and iron to molten glass.

P317   Small green glass ball on handle. Free blown. One layer. Snapped pontil mark. $5^{3/8}$"
$100.00

Blue Glass

P318   Small teal blue glass ball on handle. Free blown. One layer. Snapped pontil mark. $6^{1/4}$".
$125.00

Pottery

Although several pottery companies may have made darners, the most notable were the Cleminson Pottery of El Monte, California beginning in 1941 and the Shawnee Pottery of Zanesville, Ohio, founded in 1935. These companies made dinnerware, cookie jars, cannisters, wall vases, trays, plaques, flower pots, figurines, and pie birds.

P319   (a) Glazed pottery bowling ball shape. Hand decorated with figure, face and feet of a girl in colors of brown, green, beige, yellow and blue. Has a real ribbon bow in her hair. Marked "DARN IT." Called "The Darning Dodo" and "The Darning Dolly." Hair ribbon has been replaced. $5^{1/4}$". $45.00
(b) Another "Darning Dodo" from Cleminson pottery. Considerably different in decoration from 166a. Since they were all hand-painted, there is so much variety that collectors are known to have as many as thirty, all different. Original ribbon. $50.00
(c) Another version of Cleminson "Darning Dodo." Original ribbon. $50.00

Glass Containers

Many containers were made to be used for some other purpose, utilitarian, decorative or amusing, after the contents were used up. Candy containers were made in many shapes including cars, boats, ships, fire engines, guns, knickknacks and darners. Some used cork stoppers and some had metal screw-on caps.

P320   Blue glass ball with concave top on open ended handle. Mold blown. Embossed "AMSTER" and "Stocking Darner Pat. Apl. For." Red label with white printing reads: "Amster's Stocking Darner N.A. Amster Royersford, Pa." This darner was produced by Mr. Nehemiah A. Amster of Royersford, Pennsylvania. While employed at the Diamond Glass Company in 1913, he produced this darner in colored and clear glass, working in his spare time. His children filled the clear ones with candy pills, closed them with cork stoppers and sold them for 10 cents to stores in the surrounding towns. The colored ones were not used as candy containers but were sold simply as darners. However, they may well have been used for other purposes such as needle holders, or even as bud vases. He was granted a design patent on march 18, 1913. $5^{1/8}$". $250.00

Plate 315

Plate 316

Plate 317

Plate 318

Plate 319

Plate 320

P321 This is the green glass version of the Amster darner, minus the paper label. $225.00

P322 Blue hollow light-bulb shape with tin, cork-lined, screw-on cap. Mold blown. This is an example of a "utilitarian" container. The cork lining in the cap suggests that it was meant to be used for liquid. Which led to the theory that it could be filled with hot water on a cold winter's day to keep ones hands warm. Or filled with ice water on a hot summer day to keep you hands cool. (Or filled with brandy and forget about the weather.) $6^{1/4}$". $150.00

Glass Eggs and Handcoolers

P323 Hollow darning egg. Free blown. Cased "Spatter Glass" with orange and red spatters on a white base. Ground pontil mark. $2^{1/2}$". $85.00

P324 Hollow darning egg. Free blown. Cased "Spatter Glass" with pink and opaque gray spatters on a white base. $2^{1/2}$". $85.00

P325 Hollow darning egg. Free blown. Plum colored. Ground pontil mark. $2^{5/8}$". $70.00

P326 Solid glass egg. This is a dual purpose item, used as a "Hand Cooler" and also as a darner. $2^{5/8}$". $85.00

Spatter Glass

This is a multicolored glass incorporating several different shades in the form of particles, swirls, stripes and blazes. Although many names have been applied to it over the years, it has become most commonly known today by the generic name of "Spatter Glass."

P327 Small ball on handle. Free blown. Three layer cased, white base with spatters of green, orange, brown, blue and pink on the ball and stripes down handle. Open, polished pontil mark. $5^{1/8}$" $165.00

Plate 321

Plate 322

Plate 323

Plate 324

Plate 325

Plate 326

Plate 327

P328   Small ball on handle. Free blown. Three layer cased, white base with spatters of pink, blue and gold on ball, and swirled down handle. Open, snapped pontil mark. 5½".
$165.00

P329   Small ball on handle. Free blown. Three layer cased, white base with spatters of pink, blue, and red on the ball and swirled down the handle. Open, snapped pontil mark. 6".
$165.00

P330   Ball on handle. Free blown. Three layer cased, white base with spatters of gold, pink, green and deep blue on ball and swirled down handle. Heavy glass. Open, snapped pontil mark. 6".
$175.00

P331   Ball on handle. Free blown. Three layer cased, clear base with swirls of blue, pink, yellow, gold and white on ball and stripped down handle. Swirls are achieved by spinning the gather. Open, snapped pontil mark. 6¼".
$175.00

P332   Ball on handle. Free blown. Three layer, cased white base with spatters of pale pink, pale green and blue on the ball and swirled down the handle. Open, snapped pontil mark. 7".
$175.00

P333   Ball on handle. Free blown. Three layer cased, white base with swirls of blue, pink, yellow and a trace of gold on ball, striping down the handle. Open, snapped pontil mark.
$195.00

P334   Large ball on handle. Free blown. Three layer cased, white base with large spatters of orange, pink, green and blue on ball and striped down handle. Open, snapped pontil mark. 6¾".
$195.00

P335   Ball on bulbous handle. Free blown. Two layer cased, clear base marvered with mottling of blue and maroon on ball and swirled down handle. Open, snapped pontil mark. 6¾".
$195.00

Plate 328   Plate 329

Plate 330

Plate 331

Plate 332

Plate 333

Plate 334

Plate 335

P336   Very large ball on handle. Free blown. Three layer cased on white base with spatters of pink, blue, gold and green on ball and striped down handle. Open, ground pontil mark. 7 1/8". $195.00

P337   Large ball on handle. Free blown. Three layer cased on white base with spatters of green, blue, and pink on ball and swirled down handle. Open, snapped pontil mark. 7 1/8". $195.00

P338   Large egg on handle. Free blown. Three layer cased, white base with stylized floral design in blue, pink, orange, green, brown, yellow with stems swirled down handle. Open, snapped pontil mark.. Egg shaped darner on handle in glass is very rare. 7". $275.00

P339   Large ball on handle. Free blown. Three layer cased on white base with spatters of blue, ruby and green on ball and swirling down handle. Open, snapped pontil mark. This is Sandwich glass and an almost exact duplicate of a darner in the Sandwich Glass museum in Sandwich, Massachusetts described as:

            "SOCK DARNER
            Sandwich
            ca 1870

Blown: opaque white glass marvered with pieces of blue, green and ruby glass. This piece descended in the Brady family of Sandwich glass makers. The technique for "spattered glass" was referred to in an account of the company history written by Charles C.P. Waters in 1875. He describes how colored cullet was rolled or marvered onto the hot gather to create the spattered effect." Fragments of spattered glass have been dug at the factory site of the Boston and Sandwich Glass Company. Gertrude Whiting writes in Old Time Tools & Toys of Needlework "In an old-time New England workbag one might be lucky enough to find a salesman's traveling sample [darner] of early Sandwich glass - a rain-bow- speckled affair intended to show all the colors manufactured by his firm." 7 5/8". $250.00

P340   Ball on large, bulbous handle. Free blown. Three layer cased, white base with spatters of pink and blue on top one-third of ball. Remainder of ball and handle are not spattered. Open, snapped pontil mark. From Sandwich, Massachusetts, attributed to the Boston and Sandwich Glass Company. 7 5/8". $250.00

P341   Large ball on bulbous handle. Heavy, thick glass. One layer of clear glass marvered with swirls of blue, white and green. Ground pontil mark. Wheaton glass. $195.00

Plate 336

Plate 337

Plate 338

Plate 339

Plate 340

Plate 341

141

P342 Ball on handle. Cased. Mottled with blue and maroon, twisted down handle. Snapped pontil mark. $195.00

P343 "Door knob" style on bulbous handle. Free blown. Three layer cased clear glass with red, yellow and blue spatter on knob, swirled down handle. Closed, polished pontil mark. Czechoslovakian glass. $4_{5/8}$". $195.00

Correia Glass

Steven V. Correia is acclaimed by some as the successor to Tiffany. Correia pieces are included in the permanent collections of the Metropolitan Museum of Art, the Smithsonian Institute, the Corning Museum and the Chrysler Museum of Art.

P344 Ball on handle. With proper knop. Free blown. Cased, with dusty rose base and gold "pulled feather" design. In the style of the Correia "Iridescent Gold Ruby Collection." Signed "Correia." 7". $450.00

P345 Ball on handle with proper knop. Free blown. Cased, with black base with silver swirls and spangles. Correia calls this pattern "Zipper." In the style of the Correia "Black and Silver Collection." Signed "Correia." 7". $450.00

Steuben Glass

The Steuben Glass Works was founded in Corning, New York in 1903 by Thomas Hawkes and Frederick Carder as the artistic director. They were one of the most noted makers of a type of colored glass called Art Nouveau, along with Tiffany and Durand. The name "Steuben" came from Steuben County in which Corning is located, which in turn was named for the Prussian General Baron Friedrich Wilhelm Rudolph Gerhard Augustin von Stueben who aided General George Washington at Valley Forge. In 1918 Stueben Glass works became the Steuben Division of Corning Glassworks, and by 1933 had ceased making art glass, concentrating on the clear crystal for which they are noted today.

P346 Ball on true baluster handle with proper knop. Free blown. Single layer. Open, snapped pontil mark. This is a Frederick Carder glass known as "Green Jade." This is a typical Steuben shape, however, because darners were not a Steuben "production" item but rather were blown by individual glass blowers as whimseys. The shapes of some darners attributed to Steuben may vary somewhat. $6_{7/8}$". $500.00

P347 Ball on cylinder handle with ball knop. Free blown. Single layer. Open, ground pontil mark. This is a glass developed by Frederick Carder called "Rouge Flambe" or "flaming red." This glass was very difficult to produce. Timing and temperature had to be precise. Too much heat turned it brown. This most common position is that Stueben made Rouge Flambe for only a couple of years in 1916 and 1917, although some pieces were produced after Steuben became part of Corning Glass Works in 1918. A Rouge Flambe bowl in the Rockwell Museum is dated ca 1926. This darner may have been made in the 1920's. $6_{5/8}$". $600.00

Plate 342

Plate 343

Plate 344

Plate 345

Plate 346

Plate 347

P348   Ball on true baluster handle. Free blown. Single layer. Open, snapped pontil mark. This is another Carder glass called "Gold Aurene" and is the first art glass developed at Steuben Glass Works, in 1904. The name is from AU which is the chemical symbol for gold, which derived from the Roman name for a gold coin. The Aurene glasses, along with others such as Rouge Flambe are sometime referred to as "Reactive Glass" because the color is a reaction to the amount of heat utilized. $6^{3/4}$". $550.00

P349   Ball on true baluster handle. Free blown. Single layer. Open, snapped pontil mark. This is a Steuben glass called "Blue Aurene," another iridescent metallic Frederick Carder glass introduced in 1905. $600.00

THINGS USED AS DARNERS

One of the common things used in place of a darner was the darnee's own hand, either as a fist, or with the fingers and thumb spread to hold the stocking taut. Listed here are some of the other articles used as darners, the drinking glass and the light bulb being the most familiar shown in P350.

Nest Eggs

P351   (a) White glass. "Chicken size." Free blown. Closed, ground pontil mark. $2^{3/8}$". $7.50

(b) White glass. "Duck size." Free blown. Ground pontil mark with pin hole opening. $2^{7/8}$". $10.00

P352   (a) White glass. "Goose size." Free blown. Closed, ground pontil mark, $2^{7/8}$". $12.50

(b) White glass. "Turkey size." Free blown. Closed, ground pontil mark. $3^{1/2}$". $15.00

Gourds

P353   (a) Small, brown, egg-shaped gourd. $2^{1/2}$". $4.00

(b) Brown gourd with long neck. 6". $6.00

(c) Small, yellow gourd with short neck. 3". $5.00

Plate 348

Plate 349

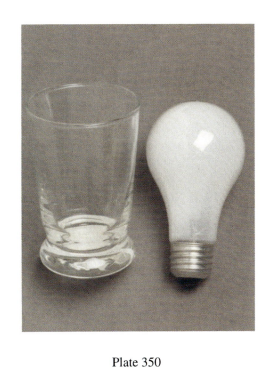
Plate 350

Plate 351

Plate 352

Plate 353

Bottle Stoppers

P354   (a) Small oblate shpere on handle. Dark green glass. Free blown. Closed, ground pontil mark. $3^{3/8}$". $10.00

(b) Small ball on handle. Clear glass with bubbles. Free blown. Open, snapped pontil mark. $3^{7/8}$". This article appears to be quite old. The presence of bubbles, sometimes called "seeds," suggests that the glass blower could not raise the furnace heat high enough to eliminate air trapped in the raw materials. $15.00

(c) Small ball on handle. Green glass. Free blown. Ground pontil mark with pin hole opening. $3^{7/8}$". $12.50

Fish Net Floats

P355   (a) Large ball. Light blue glass. Free blown. Flattened pontil plug. 3". $7.00

(b) Small ball. Amber glass. Free blown. Flattened pontil plug. 2". $5.00

(c) Large ball. White, translucent glass. Free blown. Flattened clear glass pontil plug. $2^{7/8}$". $7.00

Pestles

P356   Short true baluster shape pestle with oblate knop at end on handle. Brown stained and varnished oak. 4". $9.00

P357   Solid glass "door knop" pestle on true baluster handle with proper knop on end. Free blown. Ground pontil mark. Appears to be very old glass with small bubble imperfection "seeds" throughout. From Vienna, Austria. 6". $25.00

P358   Tapered head on long handle with small annular knop. Unfinished maple wood. $8^{3/8}$". $10.00

P359   Pear shaped head on bulbous grooved handle. Unfinished maple wood. $7^{7/8}$". $10.00

Plate 354

Plate 355

Plate 356

Plate 357

Plate 358

Plate 359

Insulators

P360   Electrical insulator. Mottled brown procelain. $3^{1/4}$". $5.00

Egg Cups

P361   White opaque "milk glass" egg cup with small and large cups. Mold blown. $4^{3/8}$".
    $7.50

Egg on Pedestal

P362   White glass egg on a short pedestal. Mold blown. Ground mold marks. From Fenton Art Glass. $3^{3/8}$". $12.50

Doorknobs

P363   White porcelain on cast iron collar. $4.00

Toy Top

P364   Wooden, egg-shaped toy top stained green. From Switzerland, where it is called a "suri." 3". $5.00

Glass Gather

P365   Very thick blue glass enlongated egg shape. This is a "gather" of glass, which is the blob of molten "metal" taken from the furnace on the end of the blowing rod. The "gaffer" had started to blow an object, possibly a bottle, and then for some reason decided not to continue and snapped it off. Probably from the Lancaster, NY medicine bottle factory. $3^{3/4}$".
    $5.00

Plate 360

Plate 361

Plate 362

Plate 363

Plate 364

Plate 365

Auto Knitter Accessory

P366   Inverted "umbrella" made of brass. Has 41 fingers that open when device on handle is pulled down. This apparatus was used with the Auto Knitter, manufactured by the Auto Knitter Hosiery Company of Buffalo, New York. The Auto Knitter was a hand operated machine that claimed to be "Better Than a Hundred Hands" when it came to knitting socks. This acccessory was used as a stocking darner also, inasmuch as the 41 fingers served to stretch the stocking in the manner of a drinking glass. Ca 1900. $6^{1/2}$". $65.00

Paper Weights

P367   (a) Small bee hive shaped paper weight containing a red and black flower. $7.50

        (b) Small round paper weight with red, white and yellow design. $7.50

Sea Shells

P368   Spotted cowrie shell $5.00

Coconuts

P369   The legendary "immature coconut." $5.00

Potatoes

P370   Nature's own darner - the potato $0.25

Plate 366

Plate 367

Plate 368

Plate 369

Plate 370

Acknowledgments

The path of research is a complex, convoluted coil of twists and turns, detours and deadends, forks and fences that no thinking person would set out to travel alone. It was so commonplace that it was taken for granted and very little of its history was documented. Researching darners is comparable to panning for gold. One washes a great deal of gravel, to find a few flecks of information.

That's why recognition is due the hundreds of people who personally contributed their knowledge and expertise to the authentication of this book. This noble group includes:

> Antique collectors
> Antique dealers
> Editors
> Writers
> Historians
> Researchers
> Librarians
> Curators
> Hosiery manufacturers
> Darner manufacturers
> Wood turners
> Wood workers
> Glass makers
> Glass blowers
> Potters
> Silversmiths
> Plastic manufacturers
> Sewing machine manufacturers
> Thread manufacturers
> Notions manufacturers
> Notions distributors
> Retailers
> Book sellers
> Patent office workers

and folks who learned about darning, who actually darned, and in some cases who still darn.

****

Marny Ashburne, East West Natural Health, The Guide to Well-Being, Brookline Village, MA.
Liz Ashford, Burlington Industries, Inc., Greensboro, NC.
Marion Ashmore, antiques dealer, Redwood City, CA.
Olga Babyak, antiques dealer, Hawthorne, CA.
John S. Bakalar, Rand McNally & Company, Skokie, IL.
Allan Bergevin, Valley Barn Antiques, author, Lakeland, MN.
Jeffrie Berline, Dritz Corporation, Spartanburg, SC.
G. Drummond Birks, Henry Birks & Sons Limited, Montreal, Canada.
Barbara Bowman, Singer Sewing Company, Edison, NJ.
Rebecca Brooke, *The Magazine Antiques,* New York, NY.
Steve C. Brown, C.A. Brown, Inc., Cranston, RI.
Shirley Brown, Shirley Brown Antiques, Poway, CA.
Emily M. Capin, collector.
Emmett Chisum, Research Historian, University of Wyoming, Laramie, WY.
Pamela Clabburn, Collector/Author, Norwich, England.
Betty Cleminson, Cleminson Pottery.
Kevin Clemens, Michelin Tire Corporation, Greenville, SC.
Miss Lisa A. Compton, Old Colony Historical Society, Taunton, MA.
Billie M. Connor, Subject Department Manager, Science, Technology & Patents Department, Los Angeles Public Library, Los Angeles, CA.
Jeannine Connor, collector/author.
Steven V. Corrreia, glass designer, Steven V. Correia Design, Topanga, CA.
Susan P. Curtis, Simplicity Pattern Co., Inc., Niles, MI.

Johan De Praeter, Susan Bates, Chester, CT.
Janice Derrick, dealer/collector, Oak Park, IL.
Doug Dezso, Candy Container Collectors of America, Maywood, NJ.
Rose A. Durand, Henry Birks & Sons Limited, Montreal, Canada.
Janean S. Edelburg, Fiskars Manufacturing Corp., Wausau, WI.
Robert Epstein, Ph.D., psychotherapist/author, Berkely, CA.
Dickey Everson, collector.
Harry F. Fischer, Acme Metal Good Manufacturing Company, Newark, NJ.
Leonard Florence, Wallace-International Silver Company, East Boston, MA.
J. Peter Fobare, Sr., Oneida Silversmiths, Oneida, NY.
Ruth A. Forsythe, collector/author.
Beryl Frank, researcher/writer.
D. Fuchs, Jobin of Switzerland, Brienz, Switzerland.
Robert Gelbstein, Eastern Silver Company, New York, NY.
Duane Gilbert, Gilbert Mfg. Corp., Locke Mills, ME.
Warren Goldfeder, Birmingham Silver Company, Yalesville, CT.
Sherry Onna Handlin, Butterick Company, Inc., New York, NY.
Keith Hanson, Henry Wilward & Sons Warwickshire, England.
Anne Holbrook, Gorham Corporation, Mount Kisco, NY.
Mrs. S. A. Hornsby, The Patent Office, London, England.
John D. Hurley, Dritz Corporation, Spartanburg, SC.
Mildred B. Jarvis, collector/author.
Robert M. Johnston, Sterling Silversmiths Guild of America, Baltimore, MD.
Lon Knickerbocker, collector/author.
E. Lkoelbl, American Woodworking Co., Montello, WI.
Ralph & Terry Kovel, Antiques Inc., Shaker Heights, OH.
Keith Lauer, collector/plastics authority, Leominster, MA.
Ann Law, collector/dealer.
Bernard T. Lee, Needle Industries Ltd., lecturer, Worcesterhire, England.
Dick Logger, Ancient Times Antiques, Laguna Nigel, CA.
Jesse Lourenco, Rosemar Silver Company, North Dighton, MA.
Marge Lucansky, Hollywood Limited Editions, Lincolnwood, IL.
James H. Lunt, Lunt Silversmiths, Greenfield, MA.
Cynthia Mace, Montgomery Ward, Chicago, IL.
Paul N. Mackey, Dritz Corporation, Spartanburg, S.C.
Lynn MacLean, Jaclyn Antiques/Books, Chatsworth, CA.
Sara C. Maness, Kayser-Roth Corp, Burlington, NC.
Joan Martin, China Tradres, Simi Valley, CA.
William D. Matthews, Oneida Silversmiths, Oneida, NY.
Maria F. Maynard, Reed & Barton Silversmiths, Taunton, MA.
Michael S. Mchale, McHale Silver, dealer/author, Los Angeles, CA.
Richard B. Miller; Baker, McMillan Co., Stow, OH.
Vincent Mongelli, Empire Silver Company, Brooklyn, NY.
Earnestine Monk, United States Department of Commerce, Patent and Trademark Office, Washington, DC.
Dale L. Murschell, author.
Mrs. Marian Noble, collector/author.
Susan Oppenheimer, Science Subject Specialist, State of California Answering Network, SCAN, Los Angeles, CA.
Loretta Patakas, Lincoln Fabrics, Venice, CA.
Jack K. Paquette, Owens-Illinois, Inc., Toledo, OH.
Marjorie Perkins, collector/author.
Joan Peterson, collector.
Ernest L. Pettit, The Tin Man, author/lecturer.
Jack Pommaney, Coats & Clark, Inc., Greenville, SC.
Donna S. Potts, Du Pont Fibers, High Point, NC.
Patricia H. Rich, collector.
Diane Richardson, dealer, Oak Park, IL.
Louise Ross, House of Fabrics, Santa Monica, CA.
Lynne Rohmerien, Curtis Archives, Indianapolis, IN.
Carolee Rowse, The Textile Museum, Washingotn, DC.
Jeff Sammartino, glass blower, Contemporary Art Glass, Millville, NJ.

Bruce J. Saunders, Saunders Brothers, Westbrook, ME.
Eileen M. Saunders, dealer, Dorset, England.
Deiter "Pete" Schlosser, wood master craftsman, Cabinetry Unlimited, Santa Monica, CA.
Jean Scottt, collector, Dorset, England.
Janice Seligman, collector/lecturer.
L.F. Smith, Kmart Corporation, Troy, MI.
B.H. Stebbins, Newell Company, Evanston, IL.
Rodney G. Stieff, Kirk Steiff Silversmiths, Baltimore, MD.
Eric van Dormolen, Bogert & Hopper, Huntington, NY.
Mort Weisenfeld, A.H. Cohen & Sons (silversmiths), Plainview, NY.
Gary White, Whites Collectibles, Oregon.
Karen White, Touch Stone Antiques, Atascadero, CA.
Tim R. Wiese, Brown Wood Products Co., Northfield, IL.
Susan Wilson, Antique Collectors Club, Suffolk England.
Catherine Yronwode, collector/author/authority on plastics.
Estelle Zalkin, collector/author.

Museums
The Abby Aldrich Rockerfeller Folk Art Center, Williamsburg, VA, Barbara R. Luck, Curator Paintings and Textiles.
The Adams House, Quincy, MA, Judy Curtis, curator.
The Baltimore Museum of Art, Baltimore, MD, Cynthia Green.
The Bucks County Historical Society, Mercer Museum, Doylestown, PA, Cory M. Amsler, Curator of Collections.
Burlington County Historical Society, Burlington, NJ.
The Colonial Williamsburg Foundation, Williamsburgh, VA, Linda Baumgarten, Curator of Textiles.
The Corning Museum of Glass, Corning, NY, Jane Shadel Spillman, Curator of American Glass.
Chester County Historical Society, West Chester, PA, Margaret Bleecker Blades, Museum Curator.
The Chrysler Museum, Norfolk, VA.
DAR Museum, Washington, DC, Mrs. Alden O'Brein, Assistant Curator of Costume. Cricket Bauer, musuem associate.
Germantown Historical Society, Philadelphia, PA, Barbara W. Silberman, Assistant Director.
The Historical Glass Museum, Redlands, CA, Lee Brandel, Docent.
House of Seven Gables, Salem, MA, Stephen J. Schier, Curator.
The Jones Museum of Glass & Ceramics, Sebago, ME, Dorothy Lee Jones, Curator.
The Library of Congress, Humanities and Social Sciences Divison, Washington, DC, L Kotzendorfer.
Mount Vernon Ladies Association of the Union, Mout Vernon, VA.
Museum of American Glass, Colonial Wheaton Village, Millville, NJ, Gay LeCleire Taylor, Curator.
The National Gallery of Art, Washington, DC, Christopher With, Coordinating Curator, Art Information Section, Department of Education Resources.
The National Plastics Center and Museum, Leominster, MA, Valerie A. Wilcox, Executive Director.
Newark Museum, University Heights, Newark, NJ. Ulysses G. Deitz, Curator Decorative Arts.
Paley Design Center, Philadelphia, PA, Arlene W. Rosenthal, Assistant Curator of Costumes.
The Rockwell Museum, Corning, NY, Robert Rockwell III, Associate Curator.
The Franklin D. Roosevelt Library and Museum, Hyde Park, NY, Alicia Vivona, Curator.
Sandwich Glass Museum, Sandwich, MA, Kirk J. Nelson, Curator of Glass.
The Shaker Museum, Old Chatham, NY, Jerry Grant, Assistant Director for Collections and Research.
Smithsonian Institution, Naitonal Museum of American History, Washington, DC, Doris Bowman, Curator of Textiles; Val Child, Sewing Tools Docent.
The Textile Museum, Washington, DC, Carolee Rowse, Library Assistant.
The University Museum, University of Pennsylvania, Philadelphia PA, Chrisso Boulis, Assistant Registrar, Records.
Valentine Museum, Richmond, VA, Colleen Callahan, curator; Ann Hedges, assistant.
Victoria and Albert Museum, London, England, Linda Woolley, Assistant Curator, Textile Furnishings and Dress.
The Henry Francis du pont Winterthur Museum, Winterthur, DE, Deborah E. Kraak, Associate Curator in Charge of Textiles.

Libraries
Los Angeles Central Library, Los Angeles, CA.
Pacific Palisades Library, Pacific Palisades, CA.
Beverly Hills Library, Beverly Hills, CA.
University of California, Santa Barbara, Romaine Trade Catalog Collection.

Others
British Consulate-General, Los Angeles, CA.

Bibliography

About Darning Eggs. Linda Gordanier Jary; Sampler and Antique Needlework Quarterly, Volume II, 1991.
Abridgments of Specifications relating to Lace-Making, Knitting, Netting, Braiding, and Plaiting; The Commissioners of Patents Sale Department; London, England. 1879.
Abridgments of Specifications Relating to Sewing and Embroidering; Office of the Commissioners of Patents for Inventions; London, England. 1871.
American Beleek Thimbles; Mildred Jarvis; TCI Bulletin, Thimble Collectors International.
American Ceramics; Garth Clark; Abbeville Press, NY. 1987.
American Glass; Georges & Helen McKearin, 1941, 1948, Crown Publ., NY.
American Glass & Glass Making; Lura (Woodside) Watkins; Chanticleer Press, NY 1950.
Antique and Collectible Thimbles and Accessories; Averil Mathis; Collector Books Div. of Shroeder Publishing Co., Inc., Paducah, KY 1986.
Antique Spoons; Victor Houart; Souvenir Press, London, England.
Antiques and Current Prices -10th Edition; Edward G. Warman; E.G. Warman Publishing Inc., Uniontown, PA. 1970.
Antiques at Home; Barbara Milo Ohrback; Clarkson N. Potter, Inc., Publisher. NY 1989.
Antiques in Their Periods, 1600-1830; Hampden Gordon, C.B.; John Murray, London. WI 1952.
Antiques of American Childhood; Katharine Morrison McClinton; Clarkson N. Potter, Inc., Publisher, NY 1970.
The Antiques Journal; July, 1972; June, 1974.
Art Glass Nouveau; Ray & Lee Grover; Charles Tuttle, Publ. Rutland, VT. 1967.
The Art of Wood Turning; Bill Poese; The Antiques Journal, July 1972.
The Book of a Thousand Thimbles; Myrtle Lundquist; Wallace-Homestead Book Co., Des Moines, IA.
The Boston Store catalogue; Boston, MA. 1898.
Butler Brothers catalogue; NY 1903, 1908.
By Shaker Hands; June Sprigg; Alfred A. Knopf, NY 1975.
Cambridge Glass 1818 to 1888, The Story of the New England Glass Company; Lura Woodside Watkins; Marshall Jones, Co., Boston, MA 1930.
Catalogue of American Antiques; William C. Ketchum, Jr.; Rutledge Books, NY 1977.
The Centennial Exposition; JS Ingram; Hubbard Brothers. 1876.
Ceramic, Furniture & Silver Collector; Edwin Atlee Barber. 1976.
Clothes Through the Ages; Mark Labovitch; Quality Press, Ltd., London. 1944.
Collecting American Victorian Antiques; Katherine Morrison McClinton; Charles Scribner's Sons, NY 1966.
Collecting Georgian and Victorian Crafts; June Field FRSA; Charles Scribner's Sons, NY 1973.
Collector's Dictionary of Glass; E.M. Elville; Country Life Ltd. Publ. London, England.
Collector's Encyclopedia of Antiques; Phoebe Phillips; Crown Publishing. 1973.
Collector's Guide to Antique American Glass; Marvin D. Schwartz: Doubleday & Co. Inc., Garden City, NY.
The Collector's Manual; N. Hudson Moore; Tudor Publishing Co., NY. 1905 Butterick Publishing Co., Ltd.
The Collector's Pocket Book of Glass; Geoffery Wills; Hawthorne Books Inc., NY 1966.
Collector's Source Book; Ralph & Terry Kovel; Crown Publishers, NY
Coloured Glass; Derek C. Davies/Keith Middlemas; 1968.
Comb Making in America; Bernard W. Doyle; Viscoloid Company, Inc.; Leominster, MA; 1925.
The Coming Collecting Boom; John Mebane; AS Barnes & Co., South Brunswick and NY 1968.
The Complete American Glass Candy Containers Handbook; George Eikelberner & Serge Agadjanian; Bowden Publishing, Mentor, OH.
The Complete Book of Needlecraft; Ida Riley Duncan; Liverith Publishing Corp., NY 1949, 1961.
The Complete Book of Small Antiques Collecting; Katharine M. McClinton; Coward-McCan, Inc., NY 1965.
The Complete Encyclopedia of Needlework; Therese de Dillmont; Running Press, Philadelphia, 1972.
The Connoisseur Illustrated Guides-Glass; Ruth Hurst Vose; The Connoisseur, London, 1975.
Concise Encyclopedia of American Antiques; Helen Comstock; Hawthorne Books Inc., NY.
Country Living, December 1984; Old Sewing Implements, Dottie M. Shaw.
Czechoslovakian Art Glass; Bill and Ellen Foster; Antiques and Collectibles, Early March 1988.
Darning Egg of Yesterday; Beryl Frank; Thimble Collector's International Bulletin, April 1987.
<u>The Days of Holly Hobbie: A Cricket Book</u>; Platt & Munk Publ., NY 1977.
Decorative Victorian Glass; Cyril Manley; Van Nostrand Reinhold Co., NY 1981.
A Dictionary of American Antiques; Carl W. Drepperd; Charles T. Branford Co., Publishers, Boston, MA 1952.
Dictionary of Antiques; George Savage; Praeger, NY 1970.
A Dictionary of Marks; Margaret MacDonald-Taylor; Hawthorne Books Inc. NY 1962.
Dictionary of World Pottery and Porcelain; Louise Ade Boger; Scribner, NY 1971.
A Directory of American Silver Pewter and Silver Plate; Ralph & Terry Kovel; Crown Publishers, NY.

Domestic Art in Women's Education, for the Use of Those Studying the Method of Teaching Domestic Art and Its Place in the School Curriculum; Anna Maria Cooley; C. Scribner's Sons, NY 1911.
Du Pont Magazine; EI Du Pont de Nemours & Co., Inc.; Wilmington Del., March 1919, February 1928; April 1929.
Eighteenth Annual Illustrated Catalogue and Price List of A.C. Becken Co.; Chicago, IL 1909.
Encyclopedia of American Silver Manufacturers; Dorothy T. Rainwater; Crown Publishers, NY 1975.
Encyclopedia of Collectibles; Time Life Books, Alexandria, VA.
Encyclopedia of Pottery and Porcelain, 1800-1960; Elisabeth Cameron; Facts on File Publ., NY 1986.
Family Circle, September 20, 1977; How to Darn.
The Forgotten Household Crafts-Trash or Treasures; John Seymour; Alfred Knopf, New York, 1987.
A Fortune in the Junk Pile; Dorothy H. Jenkins; Crown Publishers Inc., NY 1963.
WM. H. Frear & Co.'s Catalogue, Spring and Summer, 1903.
From Broad Glass to Cut Crystal; D.R. Guttery; Leonard Hill [Books] Ltd. 1956.
From Top Hats to Baseball Caps, From Bustles to Blue Jeans: Why We Dress the Way We Do; Lila Perl; Clarion Books, NY 1990.
Gifts of Distinction, Horace Anderson's Giftcraft, 1948-49.
Glass; George Savage; Octopus Books Ltd., London, England, 1972.
Glass, A Guide for Collectors; Gabriella Gros-Galliner; Stein and Day, NY 1970.
Glass Blowing - A Search for Form; Harvey K. Littleton, Van Nostrand Reinhold Co., NY 1971.
Glass Bottles, Lamps & Other Objects; Jane Shadel Spillman; Alfred A. Knopf. 1983.
Glass From Antiquity to the Renaissance; Giovanni Mariacher, translated from Italian by Michael Cunningham; The Hamlin Publishing Group Ltd, London/NY 1970.
Glass Its Tradition and Its Makers; Ada Polak; C.P. Putnam's Sons, NY
Goldsmiths & Silversmiths; Hugh Honour; G.P. Putnam's Sons, NY 1971.
A Guide to Artifacts of Colonial America; Ivor Noel Hume; Alfred A. Knopf, Inc. 1969.
Hand or Simple Turning Principles and Practice; John Jacob Holtzapffel; Dover Publications, NY 1881/1976.
The Heritage of Dress; Being Notes on the History and Evolution of Clothes; Wilfred Mark Webb; The Times Book Club, London. 1912.
History of Hand Knitting; Richard Rutt; B.T. Batsford Ltd, London. 1987.
A History of the Machine-Wrought Hosiery and Lace Manufacturers; William Felkin. 1867.
History of Needlework Tools and Accessories; Sylvia Groves; London, Country Life. 1966.
The Horizon Book of the Middle Ages; Norman Kotker in charge; Morris Bishop, author; American Heritage Publishing Co., Inc., NY.
Hosiery Through the Years; Ira Joesph Haskel; Carole Mailing Service, Lynn, MA 1956.
Illustrated Dictionary of Pottery; George Savage; Praeger, NY
The Illustrated Guide to American Glass; Emma Papert; Hawthorne Books Inc., NY.
Illustrated Guide to American Makers and Marks; Dorothy T. Rainwater; Crown Publishers Inc., NY.
Illustrated History of Needlework Tools; Gay Ann Rogers; Needleworks Unlimited, Claremont, CA 1983. John Murry Ltd., London. 1983.
The Importance of Wearing Clothes; Lawrence Langner; Hastings House, NY 1959.
The Jewelers Circular-Keystone Sterling Flatware Pattern Index; a Chilton Publication; Radnor, PA
The Knopf Collector's Guide to American Antiques: Silver and Pewter; Alfred A. Knopf. Inc., NY.
Know Your Collectibles: Ralph & Terry Kovel; Crown Publishers, Inc. NY.
Kovels' Antiques & Collectibles Price List 9th Edition, 12th Edition, 16th Edition, 20th Edition, 21st Edition, 23rd Edition, 24th Edition, 25th Edition; Ralph and Terry Kovel; Crown Publishers, Inc., NY.
Kovels' Guide to Selling Your Antiques and Collectibles; Ralph and Terry Kovel; Crown Publishers Inc., NY 1987.
S.S. Kresge, Kresge's Katalog, 1915.
The Language of Fashion; Mary Brooks Picken; Funk & Wagnalls Co., NY/London. c1939.
Lenox Belleek; Lenox, Inc.; Trenton, NJ; 1909.
Lewis & Conger catalogue, 1940.
Life Magazine, July, 1943.
R.H. Macy & Company catalogue, NY 1909.
Masterpieces of Glass; Robert J. Charleston; Harry N. Abrams Inc., Pub., NY.
Measured Drawings of Shaker Furniture & Woodenware: Ejner Handberg; Berkshire Traveller Press, Stockbridge, MA. 1980.
Mend It: A Complete Guide to Clothes Repair; Maureen Goldsworthy; Stein and Day, NY. 1979.
The Mender's Manual; Estelle J. Foote, MD; Harcourt Brace Jovanovich, NY/London. 1976.
Miller's International Antiques Price Guide; Judith & Martin Miller; Viking Studio Books, NY 1992.
Miller's World Encyclopedia of Antiques; Judith & Martin Miller; Viking Studio Books, NY.
Montgomery Ward & Co.'s Catalogues, Chicago, IL. 1893-1933.
The National Trust Book of Forgotten Household Crafts; John Seymour, Dorling Kindersley, London 1987.
Neat and Tidy; Nina Fletcher Little; E.P. Dutton, NY. 1980.
Needlework in America; Virginia Churchill Bath; Viking, NY 1979.
Needlework Tools: a Guide to Collecting; Eleanore Johnson; Shire Publications Ltd.; London, England. 1966.
Needlework Tools and Accessories; Sylvia Groves; Country Life Ltd.; London, England. 1966.

Needlework Tools and Accessories-A Collectors Guide; Molly Proctor; B.T. Batsford, London, England, 1990.
The Needleworkers' Dictionary; Pamela Clabburn; William Morrow & Company, Inc., New York. 1976.
New Clothes: What People Wore, From Caveman to Astronauts; Lisle Weil; Atheneum, NY 1987.
The New Encyclopedia of Modern Sewing, Life Savers; Frances Blondin; Wm. H. Wise, NY 1946.
Nineteenth Century Art Glass; Ruth Webb Lee; M. Barrows & Co., Inc., NY 1952.
Nineteenth Century Glass; Albert Christian Revi; Galahad Books, NY
The Official Price Guide to Antiques and Other Collectibles, Third Edition; Grace McFarland; The House of Collectibles, NY 1981.
The Official Price Guide to Sewing Collectibles, 1st Edition; Joyce Clement; The House of Collectibles, NY 1987.
Old Glass-European and American; N. Hudson Moore; Tudor Publishing Co., NY.
Old Needlework Boxes and Tools, Their Story and How to Collect Them; Mary Andere; Drake, NY. 1971.
Old Time Tools & Toys of Needlework; Gertrude Whiting; Dover Publications, Inc., NY 1971.
Old Ways of Working Wood; Alex W. Bealer; Barre Publishers, Barre, MA. 1972.
The Overlooked Egg; Marilyn Wallace Luff; The Antique Trader Weekly, January 17, 1979.
The Oxford English Dictionary; Second Edition prepared by J.A. Simpson and E.S. C. Weiner, Volume IV. Clarendon Press, Oxford, England. 1989.
Patents for Inventions, Abridgments of Specifications relating to Lace-Making, Knitting, Netting, Braiding and Plaiting; The commissioners of Patents' Sale Department, London. A.D. 1675-1866.
People Magazine. 10/14/91.
The Picture and Rhyme Book; Fern Bisel Peat; Saalfield Publ. Co. Akron, Ohio, 1941.
Pittsburgh Glass 1797-1891; Lowell Innes; Houghton-Miffin Co., Boston, MA 1976.
The Pohlson Galleries catalogue. Pawtucket, RI 1930.
The Pottery and Porcelain Collector's Handbook; William C. Ketchum: Funk and Wagnalls, NY. 1971.
Practical Needlework: An Illustrated Guide; Chartwell Books, Secaucus, NJ 1980.
Price Guide to Country Antiques and American Primitives: Dorothy Hammond: Funk & Wagnalls, NY. 1975.
Schroeder's Antiques Price Guide 5th Edition; Sharon & Bob Huxford; Collector Books, div of Schroeder Publishing Co. Inc., Paduach, KY. 1987.
Scrimshaw and Scramshanders-Whales and Whalemen; E. Norman Fladerman; N. Fladerman & Co., Inc., New Milford, CT.
Sears, Roebuck & Co., Catalogues, Chicago, IL. 1896-1949.
Sewing Accessories; Victor Houart; Souvenir Press, London. 1984.
Sewing: the Complete Guide; HPBooks, Tucson; Fisher Publishing Inc. 1983.
Shreve & Company catalogue; San Francisco, CA . 1890.
Silver in the Golden State; edited by Edgar W. Morse; The Oakland Museum History Department, Oakland, CA. 1986.
Singer Sewing Book; Gladys Cunningham; Golden Press/Div. of Western Publishing Co. Inc. 1969.
Sotheby Parke Bernet Price Guide to Antiques & Decorating Arts, 1980; Charles Colt; Simon & Schuster.
Spors Wholesale Catalogue, Spors Importing Company, Le Center, MN. 1933.
Stockings for a Queen-the Life of the Rev. William Lee, the Elizabethan Inventor; Milton and Anna Grass; A.S. Barnes & Co., Inc., Cranbury, NJ, South Brunswick and New York. 1967.
Sterling Flatware Pattern Index-Alphabetical List of American Sterling Flatware Manufacturers; Jeweler's Circular, Keystone.
STEUBEN-Seventy Years of Glass Making; Paul N. Perrot, Paul V. Gardner, James S. Plaut; Praeger Publishers, NY/Washington.
The Sure Winner price list, N. Shure Company, 1918.
Thimble Treasury; Myrtle Lundquist; Wallace-Homestead Book Co., Des Moines, IA.
Thimbles; Edwin F. Holmes; Gill and Macmillan Ltd, Dublin, Ireland.
Thomas Register of American manufacturers; Thomas Publishing Co., NY. 1994.
Trash or Treasurers - Sewing Tools; Andrea Di Noto/Dorothy Cashion; Crown Publishers, NY 1977.
Treasures of America; The Reader's Digest Association, Inc., Pleasantville, NY 1974.
Treen & Earthenware; Anne Forty; Midas Books, Speldhurst, Tunbridge Wells, Kent, England. 1979.
Treen and Other Wooden Bygones; Edward H. Pinto; Bell & Hyman, London, England. 1969.
20,000 Years of Fashion-The History of Costume & Personal Adornment; Francois Boucher; Harry N. Abrams, Inc., NY.
Two Hundred Years of American Blown Glass; Helen & George S. McKearin; Doubleday, Garden City, NY 1950, 1966.
United Sates Department of Commerce-Patent and Trademark Office.
Victoriana: A Collector's Guide; Jean Latham; Frederick Muller, Ltd., Fleet Street, London, England. 1971.
Victorian Antiques; Thelma Shull; Charles E. Tuttle Co.,; Rutland, VT. 1963.
Victorian Glass, Ruth Webb Lee; Northboro, MA. 1944.
Wallace Homestead Price Guide to Antiques and Pattern Glass, Fifth Edition; Robert W. Miller; Wallace Homestead Book Company, Des Moines, IA. 1978.
John Wanamaker Catalogue, New York. 1904.
Warman's Americana & Collectibles; Hary L. Rinker; Wallace-Homestead Book Co., Radnor, PA.
The Charles William Stores "Your Bargin Book;" NY 1914, 1918, 1923, 1928.
The Woodworkers' Bible; Percy W. Blandford; Tab Books, Blue Ridge Summit, PA.. 1979.
The Woman's Day Book of Antique Collectibles; Dorothy H. Jenkins; The Main Street Press, Pittstown, NJ 1981 CBS Publications.
World Book Encyclopedia; World Book, Inc.; A. Scott Fetzer Co. 1989.
Zalkin's Handbook of Thimbles and Sewing Implements, 1st Edition; Estelle Zalkin; Warman Publishing Co., Inc., Willow Grove, PA 1988.

Index

**WOODEN EGGS, BALLS AND PEARS ON
WOODEN HANDLES** **34-55**
    Ball shape 46-47, 52-53
    Beehive 44-45, 54-55
    Bois Noirci 36-37
    Chatelaine, part of 40-41
    Cone shape 46-47
    Ebony 36-37
    Enameled, black 34-35
    Enameled, marbleized 36-39
    Enameled, pink 40-41
    Enameled, white 40-41
    Figurals 40-43
        Flapper, City Slicker
        Vamp, Mammy
    Glove darner handle 44-45
    Harley darner 50-51
    Hollow eggs 48-51
    Lignum vitae 44-45
    Merrick darner 48-49
    Mesquite 44-45
    Mushroom 54-55
    Nodder 40-41
    Non-roll 48-49, 52-53
    Painted, blue 40-41
    Painted, green 40-41
    Paper of needles 48-49
    Pear shaped 34-35, 46-47, 52-53
    Plasticized, black 36-37
    Plasticized, pink 38-39
    Primitive 52-55
    Shaker 44-45
    Spring handle 40-41
    Unvarnished 42-43
    Varnished 42-47

WOODEN FOOT FORMS **54-57**
    Combination 56-57
    Enameled 56-57
    Natural 54-55
    On handle 56-57

**WOODEN DARNERS WITH GLOVE
DARNER HANDLES** **58-61**
    Atkinson darner 58-59
    Bell shaped 60-61
    California Big Tree 58-59
    Concave shape 60-61

**WOODEN COMPOSITES, TUNBRIDGEWARE,
STICKWARE** **60-63**
    Ball, stickware 62-63
    Ball on handle, stickware 60-61
    Dumbbell, stickware 60-61
    Egg, stickware 62-63
    Egg on handle, composite 62-63
    Egg on handle, stickware 62-63
    Glove darner handle 62-63
    Mushroom, Tunbridge 60-61
    Prison Art 62-63
    Tunbridge Wells 60

**WOODEN MUSHROOMS AND
BEEHIVES** **64-77**
    Beehive 68-69
    Cumberland Pencil Co. 68
    Garment darner 68-69
    Mushroom, bog oak 137-138
    Mushroom, Mauchline 74-75
    Mushroom, painted cottage 72-73
    Mushroom, painted floral 72-75
    Mushroom, painted red cap 70-73
    Mushroom, painted swirls 70-71
    Mushroom, painted solid color 70-71
    Mushroom, primitive 74-75
    Mushroom, printed 74-77
    Mushroom, stained 66-69
    Mushroom, varnished 66-67
    Mushroom, unvarnished 64-67

**SOLID WOODEN EGGS, BALLS, CAPSULES,
CONES, PESTLES** **76-83**
    Ball 80-83
    Boye Darning form 80-81
    Capsule 79-81
    Colored/Decorated 76-78
    Cone 80-81
    Darning form 80-81
    Egg, enameled black 76-77
    Egg, laminated 76-77
    Egg, painted swirls 76-77
    Egg, painted white 78-79
    Egg, stained purple 76-79
    Lollipop 82-83
    Mending knob 82-83
    Natural 78-79
    No-Darn knob 82-83
    Sphere, flattened 78-79
    Strumpf kugel 80

**HOLLOW EGGS, COMPENDIUMS,
THIMBLE CASES** **82-89**
    Compendium, Mauchline 84-87
    Compendium, metal, enameled 88-89
    Compendium, patented, Conrad Woge 86-87
    Compendium, Trina - Hong Kong 88-89
    Compendium, printed 88-89
    Souvenir, ... 82-85
    Hollow egg, wood 82-85
    Hollow eggs, varnished, stained, enameled 84-86
    Mauchline Tartanware 84-89
    Needle case, wood, Columbia Egg 88-89
    Scotchware 84
    Seaweed 84
    Stopfen Kugel 82
    Stopholz 82
    Tartanware 84
    Thimble case, wood 84-85
    Thimble case, wood and metal 84-85

**FABRIC HOLDER DARNERS - CLIPS, SPRINGS,
ELASTICS, BRUSHES** **90-95**
    Brush, black enameled wood with plastic brush 94-95
    Brush, Marvel darner, wire bristles 94
    Clip, black wood, patent - William Snyder 90
    Clip, varnished wood, needle holder handle 90
    Clip, varnished wood, patent - William Snyder 90
    Elastic, painted, needle holder handle 91-92
    Elastic, black wood, natural wood 92-93

Queen Stocking and Glove Darner	90
Spring, door knob, black, patent, Charles Gale	92
Spring, "Ebor," patent, John Kelley	92
Spring, mushroom	92
Spring, "The Trick," reversible	92-93
Stoppspannare	90
CELLULOID, BAKELITE, IVORY, PLASTIC	**94-101**
Bakelite	94-95
Bakelite, mushroom, hollow for storage	96-97
Celluloid	94-95
Celluloid, egg on handle	94-95
Celluloid, mushroom, red cap, needle holder	96-97
Cellulose acetate	94-95
Cellulose nitrate	94
Ivorene	94-95
Ivory, mushroom	98-99
Ivory, walrus	98-99
Marbelette	94-95
Phenyl formaldehyde	94
Plastic, beehive on handle, patent Hungerford	96
Plastic, yellow, Glista compendium	100
Plastic, foot form	98-99
Plastic, foot form, patent, Mendle	98
Plastic, mushroom, needle holder, "Jay Brand"	96-97
ODDITIES	**100-103**
Ball in Block, wood, Shaker made	100-101
Darn-A-Lite, plastic, battery powered	101-102
Pifco Electric Darner, electric darner	100-101
Singer Darner, sewing machine accessory	102-103
Tin tube, paragum Mending Paste	100-101
WOODEN EGGS ON HANDLES OTHER THAN WOOD	**102-115**
Amethyst	112
Art Nouveau	114-116
Cartouche, ebony egg	112-113
Champleve	114-115
Durgin Silver Company	110
Ebony	102
Theodore W. Foster & Bros.	106
Mandalian & Hawkins	106
Meridan Britannia Company	114
Mother of pearl handle, ebony egg	114-115
Palmer & Peckham	110
Reddall & Company	112
Shreve & Company	104-105, 112
Staghorn	112-115
Sterling silver handles	102
Sterling handle, Art Nouveau	114-115
Sterling handle, ebony egg	102-109
Sterling handle, black enameled egg	104-105
Sterling handle., composite egg	110-113
Sterling handle, green enameled egg	110-111
Sterling handle, jewelled, ebony egg	112-113
Sterling handle, maroon enameled egg	110-111
Sterling handle, white enameled egg	110-111
GLOVE DARNER	**116-119**
La Pierre Mfg. Co.	116
Silver	116-117
Webster Company	116
Wood	116-119
GLASS	**118-145**
Alabaster	120
Amber	132-135
Amster	134-135
Belleek, American	120
Blue	134-135
Botttle	132-133
Boston and Sandwich Glass Company	122
Frederick Carder	142
Cased	122, 124
Ceramic Art Co.	120
Clear	126-128
Clear with color blazes	128-129
Cleminson Pottery	134
Cobalt	130-133
Cobalt, frosted	132-133
Containers	134-137
Corriea	142-143
Corning Glass Works	130-142
Cranberry	118-121
Czechoslovakian	122-123
Draped	118
Durand	142
Eggs	136-137
Foot Forms	128-131
Green	134-135
Gunderson Glass Company	122
Hand coolers	136
Thomas Hawkes	142
Hobbs, Brockunier & Company	122
Kristl	128
Looped	118-119
Daniel Lows	128
Mercury	124
Milk	120-121
Mount Washington Glass Company	122
Mushrooms	128-129
Nailsea	118-119
New England Glass Works	122
New Martinsville Glass Company	122
Pairpoint Company	122, 130
Peachblow	122-123
Pilgrim Glass Company	118, 120
Porcelain	120-121
Pottery	134-135
Powdered	124-126
Rouge Flambe	142
Silvered	124
Spatter	136-143
Steuben,	142-145
Tiffany	130
Venetian	132-133
THINGS USED AS DARNERS	**144-151**
Auto Knitter accessory	150-151
Bottle stoppers	146
Coconuts	150-151
Door knobs	148-149
Egg cups	148-149
Fish net floats	146-147
Glass eggs	148
Glass gathers	148-149
Gourds	144-145
Insulators	148-149
Nest eggs	144-145
Paper weights	150-151
Pestles	146-147
Potatoes	150-151
Sea shells	150-151
Toy Top	148-149